Writing TV Scripts

Successful writing in 10 weeks

Aber Creative Writing Guides

The Business of Writing

The Craft of Fiction

Ghost Writing

The Writer's Glossary

Writing Crime Fiction

Writing Historical Fiction

Writing How-to Articles and Books

Writing TV Scripts

Starting to Write

Writing Soap

Writing Science Fiction

Writing and Imagery

Aber Self-Help

Choose Happiness

Write Yourself Well

Aber Money Management

Understanding the Numbers:
 the first steps in managing your money

Back to the black:
 How to get out of debt and stay out of debt

Writing TV Scripts

Successful writing in 10 weeks

Steve Wetton

www.aber-publishing.co.uk

First published in 2005 by Studymates Ltd
This edition published 2010 by Aber Publishing,
PO Box 225, Abergele, LL18 9AY, United Kingdom.

Website: http://www.aber-publishing.co.uk
Aber Publishing is a division of GLMP Ltd

ISBN: 978-1-84285-062-6

Printed and bound in the Czech Republic by Akcent Media Limited.

Contents

Foreword

I am so struck by this honest, careful, clinical and comprehensive account of how a TV script should be approached that any humorous comment of mine, however pertinent, would be out of place. Steve Wetton is so generous with his experience and research that I'm sure he would give away his talent if it were possible. There is a generosity about everything else handed out, from page margins to 'how to be persistent – repeat *persistent* –' and positive in the face of adversity. Steve came to me over 40 years ago for advice about professional writing. I was not a great deal of help as I never practised nor prepared my art, nor did I think a great deal about construction, nor dialogue, only character and theme. Somehow I worked through by instinct. I was good at dialogue, which was at a premium in those studio plays of the sixties and seventies, developments as they were of radio drama. My 'unplanned' method of organic growth – that is letting the script take you somewhere and then modifying or rejecting it – was a tortuous and often painful way to proceed. I recommend Steve's approach.

He has written to accommodate the most timorous of souls, beginning by gently lowering the reader into the warm pool of their imagination, after which they must try to swim a little. He has the reader writing – and thinking about writing – from the start. I love the times when he says 'Do it now', commands worth obeying. He builds confidence. At no time are the lessons and advice difficult to follow. Simplicity is his aim and it makes for easy and compulsive reading.

Nowadays, with film techniques employed in the making of most TV drama, there is a need to think and write with less dialogue and with a constant eye for visual presentation, though – as Steve points out – this should not be written in such a way that it dictates to the director, a golden rule.

I began writing for television in the days when playwrights were valued and their names came on screen immediately following the title. Some were more important than others. Troy Kennedy Martin, originator of the seminal series *Z-Cars*, for which series I provided a script or two, led by example. David Mercer was a literary playwright, whose themes interweaved Marxism with madness. John Hopkins wrote the jagged-edged *Talking to a Stranger*, a piece about tortured family relationships. Dennis Potter followed with his passionate plays, again with personal themes, of childhood and fantasy. I was blessed by having Innes Lloyd at the BBC drama department as my producer – he also produced all of Alan Bennett's work. Innes commissioned me to write two BAFTA winning plays, *Bomber Harris* and *Wingate.*

I doubt if Mercer, Potter or Hopkins would be writing TV today, had they lived. The world has moved on. There is no call for real playwrights any longer, only script writers, which is why Steve's book provides such valuable guidance.

I would have this on my shelf as my writer's bible, were I starting out today.

Don Shaw (creator of *Dangerfield*, BBC TV and contributor to the famous *Z-Cars* series)

Introduction

A New Approach

There have been many books written on the subject of scriptwriting for TV and some of them are excellent. This one, however, isn't just a book of information, but an instruction manual. The interactive approach is what makes this book different. It contains expert advice from someone who has not only created and written his own series for television, but who has also been conducting workshops on the subject with writers' groups and university students for many years.

Step-by-Step Guidance

You'll be writing as you go from the beginning of Chapter One onwards, but you won't be writing your actual script, or even *thinking* about doing that for at least four weeks. Until then you'll be encouraged to read the book from cover to cover and do a series of simple 'warm-up' exercises designed to improve your skills and teach you necessary information at the same time.

After the initial four weeks you'll be advised to start writing your script, as you re-read the step-by-step instructions from Chapter Seven onwards. (More details on methods of working and suggested time periods will be found at the beginning of Chapter Seven itself.)

Don't dismiss this vital initiation period. Think of yourself as someone training to be a skier. You wouldn't immediately head for an Olympic-standard ski slope and start putting yourself in competition with world-class performers. Only a maniac would do that – any sensible person would be content to start on a nursery slope.

Unfortunately, there are no nursery slopes for TV scriptwriters. The minute you send out a script you are competing with seasoned professionals as well as dozens, if not hundreds, of newcomers like yourself. Don't let this frighten you. It's not easy to write a TV script but neither is it brain surgery. Most people who want to do it give up too easily or simply don't learn enough about the process in the first place.

You may think you can save time by just reading the book for information, then ignoring the exercises and starting on your script straight away. That is entirely your prerogative, but I know from experience that, unless you've already written scripts and know a bit about the process, this will probably be a big mistake. To use another analogy, it would be a bit like pitting yourself against a top racing driver in a Formula One Grand Prix before you had even got a full driving licence.

To meet the target of writing a script in ten weeks (one that's good enough to be sent out) you might also need to give something like an average of two hours a day to this project. Obviously you don't have to do it like this. You may not have that amount of time available, in which case you can work at your own pace. Just so long as you avoid the very real danger of becoming one of the many thousands of people who are going to write a script one day, when they get around to it, but never do.

The Reasoning Behind This Book

Thousands of people watch dramas, soaps and sitcoms on television and feel they could do better if only they knew how to go about it. That's what this book is all about: turning your dreams into reality.

It is written in two parts. The first part, 'Testing the water' is all about preparation. Here you'll be learning all those things about TV scriptwriting that you think you already know but probably don't: things like how you describe characters, places and actions in a script; what actually constitutes a scene; what the writer is responsible for and, conversely, what can safely be left to others. You'll be shown what a professional script looks like and told why it needs to be set out in a particular way.

You'll be advised on how much instruction is given to actors about how to say a line and what kind of detail is needed with regard to their movements, gestures and reactions. You'll find that, unlike some other forms of creative writing like short stories or novels, very little of this comes naturally.

TV scriptwriting is a craft as well as an art, and like all crafts it has to be practised – not just learned. You'll be doing some of that practising straight away. This is supposed to be the fun part, and it will be if you approach it in the right way. You should spend about four weeks doing the exercises and absorbing the information in this section of the book.

The second section of the book, 'Taking the Plunge', gets you started on the real thing. It shows you how to set about writing your script from start to finish in a structured and efficient way. It then tells you what to do with it and what's likely to happen next.

So read the book carefully and do all the things you'll be asked to do. Then, in just ten weeks or less, you could be standing in front of a postbox with several large envelopes in your hand addressed to various people in television.

It could change your life.

The Promise of this Book

Let's make one thing clear. You're being invited to write an original thirty-minute drama or sitcom script to professional standards, an example of your work to be used as a 'calling-card'. Nobody's saying that you're likely to sell that particular script. Yes, a few people do get lucky at the first attempt, especially if the script happens to be a sitcom 'pilot' episode for a proposed series. It's happened before and will no doubt happen again, but it's unlikely.

What this book proposes is very simple: you write one well-crafted original thirty-minute television script and send copies to perhaps half a dozen producers or more (all at the same time – life's too short to wait around). You can send copies to the producers of thirty-minute series like *Eastenders* and *Doctors*, and to fifty-minute series like *Casualty*, as well as to any other series you think appropriate. There's simply no need to write a different script for each show you'd like to aim at.

Nobody will mind if your script isn't the right length or that it isn't aimed specifically at their show (in fact they might be glad it isn't). If you've actually aimed a script at a particular series and used their characters and situations without permission, some companies will return your script unread. They won't get much beyond reading your accompanying letter and glancing at the first page of your script, and won't read the actual script in case you might claim, at some future date, that they've stolen ideas from you. At this point they won't be interested in how familiar you are with *their* show, they'll just be looking for signs of definite promise they can build on.

Your initial aim is simply to gain someone's attention and perhaps be invited to write a *sample* script for their particular show, get accepted onto the writing team, and continue to learn while you earn. Creating and writing your very own world-shattering series can come later when you *really* know what you're doing.

Are the Opportunities Real?

As long as there are drama series, soaps and situation comedies being produced there will be a need for writers. That need is likely to increase as new channels appear. And already we're not talking about a handful of writers but hundreds in the UK alone. Most of those writers aren't in the genius category. They are often people with a modest talent who *understand* that scriptwriting is a craft as well as an art. They've worked at it, and if they did it so can you. It isn't brain surgery. It isn't even plumbing. Can you imagine learning much about either of those two skilled jobs in ten weeks?

Yes, you do need a certain amount of natural flair that can't be taught, and that's why not everybody can become a writer. But you must feel you already have that or you wouldn't be reading this book.

Your Most Pressing Need

Persistence. That's the one thing essential to success. You don't need to be a genius. You don't even need to be a 'good' writer – you don't need to understand the rules of grammar, have a wide vocabulary, produce vivid imagery or even write sentences that flow seamlessly from one to another, as in prose writing.

A scriptwriter doesn't have to be a good prose-writer or a poet. He or she has to be a 'natural' storyteller, someone who is fascinated by the problems of other people and is constantly trying to understand more about what makes them tick. We've all met such people. They are the ones who can make a simple incident, like missing a bus, sound like the plot from *Some Like it Hot*.

Such people might not know it but they are constantly engaged in a kind of quest; to make some sense out of life, to fit seemingly random incidents into a sort of pattern that delights or shocks us and makes us think at the same time.

Are you already one of those people? Or do you at least have the *persistence* to try and become one? Of course you'll also need various other skills to do with scriptwriting: the ability to write dialogue, make convincing scene transitions, create interesting characters, suggest interesting visuals, and so on. But these are all things that can be learned if you *persist.* It's just like riding a bicycle: you fall off – you get back on and try again.

Enough of the hard sell. Let's get on with it. Oh, and two more pressing needs: an A4 notepad and a pen or pencil. That's just for starters. If you really hope to become a professional writer you'll also need access to a computer or word processor. I hope it goes without saying that a script needs (eventually) to be printed out in a recognised format, not handwritten.

Don't worry about this at all. You'll be told more about script layout in Chapter Six, and shown exactly how to format a script to professional standards in the appendix of this book, but for now just tackle the exercises and your initial drafts in whatever way suits you best.

It makes good sense to be more concerned about content than presentation during the early stages of writing *any* script. To do otherwise would be a bit like trying to decorate and furnish a new house before the walls have been plastered.

Part One

Testing the Water

1 Easy Does It

One-minute Overview

In this chapter you'll be invited to do a simple exercise to remind yourself how much fun being creative can be. You'll then be given a brief overview of what writing scripts for TV is all about. You'll be told what the writer is responsible for – what he or she actually includes in a script – and what can safely be left to others. You'll be told a little about who does what in terms of handling your script and, most importantly, you'll be reminded that you don't have to be a genius to give it a try.

Remember what I said in the introduction: to get the best from this book you really need to read every chapter *and* do the exercises suggested. Do them in a relaxed manner. Nothing is really at stake. Unless you decide otherwise, nobody except yourself need ever know how well or how badly you are doing at this stage. The more carefree your attitude and the more mistakes you're willing to make, at first, then the more creative you will be. Just relax and enjoy yourself.

A Simple Test to Prove You Can Do It

I've based this little exercise on something I read in a wonderful book, aimed at people working in the theatre, called *Impro* by Keith Johnstone (first published in hardback by Faber and Faber in 1979, and later published by Eyre Methuen and Methuen Drama in paperback from 1981 onwards). I used it for years with my drama students when I taught in schools and found it works just as well for people who want to become scriptwriters. See what you make of this:

A: Hello
B: Hello

A: Been waiting long?
B: Yes ... ages ...
A: So. Shall we ...?
B: Why not?

(They move away.)

Nothing too difficult or complex there – at least at first glance. This could simply be two casual acquaintances meeting at a bus stop and sharing a few meaningless phrases before boarding the bus and then going their separate ways.

We've all seen dramas and comedies that start like this – that set the location in some particular city and introduce the main character – but it's lazy writing. Not only would it be pretty boring, it would also be very wasteful in terms of TV drama.

Here you have a scene that only lasts a few seconds but which could take all morning to shoot at considerable cost, and which doesn't actually do anything. As a new writer hoping to make a good first impression you'll have to do better than that.

Make a note

- In a TV script try to make every single word of dialogue count.
- Outside locations are expensive, so use them effectively.

Write these two things in your notepad now or highlight them in this book. They are very important and will be mentioned again.

In fact, it's not that difficult to make the words count and to get the most out of your location. Just imagine, for instance, that the two people in this little scene aren't casual acquaintances but total strangers, meeting for the first time for an important reason. Then give each character an attitude towards the situation. Maybe character A is assertive and character B nervous – or the other way around. Maybe they are both assertive and impatient – or both nervous and hesitant.

You can see that we've already created four totally different possibilities out of this very ordinary set-up. Now every word spoken, not to mention every gesture made, will convey some dramatic depth and meaning. And that's before we've decided whether they are male or female, young or old, meeting in a strange and exotic location or in a brightly lit office.

I'm sure that even the least confident would-be TV scriptwriter could make something of this without much help. So why not have a try? Ask yourself these questions:

Who are these two people?

Where are they?

Why are they there?

What's their attitude?

When I give you the signal I'd like you to close your eyes for a moment and let your subconscious take over. Let various ideas swirl through your mind. Don't try to force anything or take conscious decisions and don't try too hard to remember everything you've just read or to get the dialogue exactly 'right'.

Remember, this is basically two people meeting and saying a few introductory words. So relax and try to 'see' and 'hear' the scene just as it might be happening on a TV screen in front of you, or even in reality, with you as an invisible witness. Just take a minute or so – not too long – and then come back to the book. Ready?

Do it now!

How did it go? Did it come easily and quickly? Did you decide without hesitation that both characters were male, both assertive, both in their mid-thirties and meeting in a dark alleyway to plan a contract killing?

Or did you decide that one character was male and one female, both in their early forties, both timid and meeting in a brightly lit restaurant on a blind date?

Or did you become so overwhelmed by the realisation that the possibilities are infinite that you started dithering and changing your mind straight away? Not sure what age they were, what sex, where the location was and why they were there in the first place? If you did – welcome to the club. I could dither for Britain.

Whatever you came up with, it doesn't matter. You've made a start at thinking like a scriptwriter. All that really matters is the end product and that's ten weeks away. Some of us, like one of my daughters, are natural 'one-hour jugglers' and some of us, like myself, are 'six-week jugglers'. I'll explain what I mean by this later but let's continue with the exercise first.

In a moment I want you to pick up your pencil and notepad and write out the scene you imagined, or a different one if you prefer, but still about two people meeting and using those same lines of dialogue at the beginning. Now that you're actually writing it, add a few more lines of dialogue and also add visuals. Describe the location and situation, and give the characters names and ages as well as an attitude.

Don't think too deeply. Just let it flow out of the pencil as if by magic. If what you write is rubbish don't stop – keep writing. You can always alter it later. The worst thing you can do is try to get it 'just right' the first time. You could wait forever doing it that way.

As I said in the introduction to this book, don't worry about making it look like a TV script at this point. You're just doing warm-up exercises, getting your mind to show how creative it can be. Finally, don't alter it too much before you come back to this book; just let it flow, whether it's 'good', 'bad' or 'indifferent'. Don't be afraid to surprise yourself by writing something totally unexpected.

Just to remind you: two people (now with names and ages, plus an attitude towards the situation) are meeting for the first time. We need to know where they're meeting but not necessarily why. Keep the audience guessing (and yourself at this point).

Only write for ten minutes or so and then come back to the book. I'll do it too and see what happens. Are you ready?

Do it now!

Welcome back. This is how my attempt went:

> A parking area close to a ramblers' trail. An expensive car glides into a parking position and the sole occupant, an attractive woman in her early forties, Lucinda Graham, gets out. She looks totally out of place in her high-heeled shoes and designer clothes. She is agitated and impatient.
>
> A group of Hell's Angel motorcyclists are approaching along the road. Lucinda looks at them and seems relieved when they pass her by. She turns to look in another direction. She's startled by the roar of a bike engine from close behind her. She turns to see a bearded biker, Jack Thornton, in his early forties, sitting astride a huge bike.

He raises his goggles. No reaction from Lucinda. Now he peels off the false beard and gives a cynical smile. He's rugged but not bad looking. Still no reaction from Lucinda.

Jack: Hello.

Lucinda: Hello.

Jack: Been waiting long?

Lucinda: Yes ... ages ...

Jack: So shall we ...?

He indicates the empty pillion behind him and offers a helmet that's on the petrol tank in front of him. She looks at him with utter disbelief and looks down at her own clothes. He just keeps smiling and waiting as if he knows she has no choice. She walks around for a few seconds as if deciding whether or not to kill him with her bare hands. She walks to the car and wrenches the door open, but instead of getting in she turns and gives him a look of defiance.

Lucinda: Why not?

She tugs at her skirt. It comes off in one swift movement. Underneath the posh skirt she's wearing sensible shorts. Now she gives a frosty smile of triumph as she unbuttons her top. Beneath that there's a sensible blouse. She tosses the clothes and her high-heeled shoes into the car and gets out some biking leathers.

Jack: You're brighter than I thought.

Lucinda: Let's hope you're brighter than you look ...

He smiles: touché. We end the scene on Lucinda's determined look.

I have no idea why I wrote this. The contrast between a posh woman in an expensive car and a Hell's Angel on a big bike must have seemed interesting to my subconscious mind. Then the fact that she lied within seconds, saying she'd been waiting for ages when she'd only just arrived. But what's it really about? Is the woman being blackmailed? Has her daughter been kidnapped and now Lucinda is being driven somewhere remote to see her? Is Lucinda a trainee secret agent being given an initiative test? I don't know and I don't really care. It was just an exercise. I won't be following it through.

It's not the best thing I've ever written off the top of my head but it's not the worst either. If I hadn't just made it up myself, but watched it on TV, I think I'd be tempted to give it at least a few more minutes. So how did you get on with your effort? Maybe it was better than mine? If so, well done. If not, don't worry – you're learning.

Make a note	• You must give some thought to the visuals in terms of cost and effectiveness. • You must give each main character an attitude to the situation (their own agenda).

To explain the remark I made earlier about juggling – some years ago I bought one of my daughters a set of juggling balls for Christmas. On Christmas morning I found her sitting on the bed juggling away quite happily. I said that I hadn't realised she knew how to juggle. She said that neither had she until she opened the packet and found an instruction leaflet. I couldn't believe it. She had read a list of instructions and taught herself to juggle within an hour.

I said I'd have a go myself later. I did. It took me six weeks – practising every day during spare moments – to do what she had done in an hour. I had always thought I had great co-ordination (as a youngster I was quite a promising boxer, where hand speed is so important), so I was surprised and a bit humbled to see one of my teenage daughters learn something so much more easily than I could. But the really important thing is that I carried on practising and now I'm just as good as she is. I'm never going to juggle chainsaws while riding a unicycle, but I hope you get the point.

I was a six-week juggler and my daughter was a one-hour juggler, but to anybody watching us now that doesn't matter a damn. It's the end product that counts.

And it's the same with scriptwriting. No one in the industry will care how long it took you to learn the craft – ten weeks, ten months or even ten years – so long as you can do it now, and do it well enough and fast enough to meet their deadlines.

Make a note

- To other people it doesn't matter how long it took you to learn something.
- The end result is all that matters.

What's 'Different' About TV Writing?

Let's keep this brief and think about the split between dialogue and visuals, which is usually something like this:

TV: 50% dialogue/50% visual.
Film: 25% dialogue/75% visual (all that screen to be filled up).
Stage: 75% dialogue/25% visual (space and 'visual effects' restrictions).
Radio: 95% dialogue/0% visual (plus sound effects and music).

Television is interesting because it's the only one that gives a roughly even split between dialogue and visuals. You have to think visually but still pay close attention to the dialogue.

You must be aware, however, that this rarely appears obvious in the script itself. Some pages will have little dialogue and large chunks of explanatory 'directions' and other pages will have nothing *but* dialogue. This does not make a great deal of difference to the viewer because, irrespective of what's in the script, he or she will always have something to look at as well as something to listen to – even if it's just two people sitting in a small room talking.

The writer needs to be aware of this. Even if he or she has written a page that is all dialogue, there will still be something for the audience to see – and it could be just as important or even more important than what the characters are saying. Anything the audience can deduce from what they see doesn't need to be said. In terms of dialogue 'less is usually more' for the television viewer.

Let me give a few examples of this. A man picks up some newly delivered letters in the hallway of a house and shouts: 'The postman's been.' Of course he has. We can clearly see it, so it doesn't need to be said. Instead of wasting dialogue like this, have the person say something that *adds* to what we're seeing instead of just repeating it.

For example, he might nervously sort through the letters in silence and give a whispered shout of 'Yes!' before hiding one particular letter inside his dressing gown and shouting: 'Just the usual darling – bills and junk mail.' Then we've got something interesting to think about. Why is he hiding this letter from his wife or partner? Is it a love letter from another woman? An offer of a job he's applied for that could end his marriage and become the start of a new life?

Here's another example. One woman hands another woman a cup of tea and says, 'Tea, wasn't it?' This is perfectly reasonable but doesn't tell us anything to grab our interest. But suppose the woman handing over the cup is slim and elegant and the other woman is slightly overweight and less fashionably dressed. If the first woman says, 'I thought it best not to include sugar darling ...' as she gives a sly glance at her friend's figure, then we know there's some animosity between the two and that there's a promise of conflict to follow.

One of the more boring things you can do with dialogue is use it to let one character explain to another something we already know. A person has just had an argument with somebody and says to the next person they meet, 'I've just had an argument with your friend John.' Of course they have. We all saw it. It's even worse if he or she then goes on to repeat what the argument was all about. All this dialogue is wasted. It's taking up time that could be used by more efficient dialogue. Don't do it.

We'll be going into dialogue in much more detail later on but for now just remember that, if the audience can 'get' something without it being said, don't say it.

Make a note

- If something doesn't need to be said, don't say it.
- Actions speak louder than words.
- In terms of dialogue less is usually more on TV.
- Think of TV as being a 50/50 split between what we see and what we hear, even when it doesn't look like that on the page.

Just to reassure you, one thing that's special about TV is the fact that people who are good at dialogue and good at visuals but brilliant at neither can still succeed. It's an interesting balance. You don't have to excel at one thing or the other.

Who Does What in Making Shows for TV?

Throughout the book mention will be made of various people involved in the production process. It might be useful to give a brief mention to some of them straight away to avoid confusion.

Script-reader

A term used loosely, in this book, to signify whoever is reading your script. A big organization like the BBC might have people employed specifically as 'readers' but in smaller companies your script will usually be read initially by someone who is also a script-editor, a producer's assistant of some kind, or even a producer.

Script-editor

The person who will work most closely with the writer, going through the script line-by-line before it's ready to be presented to everyone else as a completed 'rehearsal script'. (The script will be called a rehearsal script until after the director adds notes on camera angles and other technical details. It will then be re-typed, by a secretary, and become a 'shooting script'. The writer isn't involved in this.)

Director

The person who actually 'directs' the actors, the cameras and the sound crew and turns your words on the page into a TV show.

Producer

The person in overall charge of the show, who has the final say over the people mentioned above (and many others). It might be useful for you to think of the producer as a head-teacher in a school, someone responsible for everything, from cleaning and catering to the curriculum. In this context you may then think of the director as a teacher, someone who just focuses on the main job at hand.

More details will be given about these various positions later on (in Chapter Twelve) but for now this should be all the information you need.

What the Writer Actually Writes

Writing a television script is very much part of a team process. If you're precious about your work, take criticisms very personally and dread the thought of somebody changing a single word, don't write TV scripts – keep a diary instead.

Of course, if you reach the stage of being invited to write an episode for an ongoing series you'll be given very strict guidelines because your episode will have to fit in seamlessly with the ones that went before and the ones that follow. You should have watched several preceding episodes but can only guess at the episodes that haven't been written yet. That's where the script editor comes in. He or she will liaise with you in this case, telling you clearly what is and what isn't possible.

But even when your script is entirely original (as your thirty-minute calling-card script should be) you must bear in mind that at some point, if it's ever considered for production, people will demand changes. Nobody ever reads a script and says, 'Brilliant. Run off twenty copies while I get the cameras in position.' It just doesn't work like that. Preparations have to be made and decisions taken, and script-editors, producers, directors and actors will all want a say in the proceedings. How much this input is beneficial to the writer is, at times, debatable but you'll have to live with it.

Just to mention one thing, it would be a very confident script-editor indeed who says that a script is perfect and doesn't need any changes – a producer might then ask the script-editor what he or she plans to do for the next few days or weeks. But you, as writer, won't know certain things that the script-editor does know. Things like:

- How much money is available for the project.
- How much location shooting there can be.
- How many sets can be built in the studio.
- How many speaking characters and extras you can use.
- How close your ideas may be to something that's already in the pipeline.

However, we're not at the stage of dealing with script-editors, directors and producers yet, so what does the writer write in the beginning? We're talking now about your original calling-card script – not a trial script for an existing show.

- The writer invents the story – with a beginning, a middle and an end.
- The writer creates the characters (describing them very briefly at first point of entry into the script – not in the cast list – but more about this later).
- The writer writes the dialogue.
- The writer (at least initially) chooses the location, the tone and the genre:
  – Is it set mainly in the back streets of Manchester or in the wilds of Scotland?
  – Is it a comedy or a tragedy?
  – Is it a murder mystery or a costume drama, etc.

It all starts with the writer. As it says in the Bible, 'In the beginning was the word.' Before the writer there is nothing but a pile of blank sheets and a bunch of people drawing jobseekers' allowance. (Okay – so I exaggerate a bit, but you get the idea? The writer is important and should always be aware of this.)

So all the things listed above are down to the writer at the beginning, but they are all liable to be altered: usually by the writer after consultation, but sometimes by other people without consultation. There's not a lot you can do about this. You've sold your script and it's no longer your property. It's a bit like selling your house and expecting the new owners to keep your purple-and-orange wallpaper and buy furniture that blends in with it.

You could ask for your name to be taken off the credits or you could, I suppose, write to every viewer in the land explaining how good your version was compared with the cock-up somebody else made of it, but by and large you take the good with the bad and keep quiet. The good news is that on balance a writer gets as much unearned credit when things go really well, as undeserved criticism when things go wrong. As I said, it's a team effort.

There are dozens of reasons for changes to be made and many of them are nothing at all to do with the quality of the writing. So expect changes and accept them willingly unless you really, really don't agree with them and have good reasons for this.

What the Writer Doesn't Write

Here are a few things the writer does not have responsibility for:

- The writer does not tell the director where to point the cameras.
- The writer does not tell the actors how to say their lines.
- The writer does not give unnecessary detail on things or people.
- The writer does not give information that can't be conveyed to the audience.

Perhaps some clarification is necessary here?

Pointing the cameras

The writer says *what* we see but not *how* we see it. So we see two people sitting at a table talking in a restaurant and the situation is explained very briefly. 'Tom and Pat are seated at one of the tables.' Then we get the dialogue.

A good director will vary the visuals, perhaps using three cameras and maybe starting with both people in the frame and giving us a view of the size of the place and a sample of other customers or staff. Then we might go to another camera for a close-up of just one person talking and then flick over to the third camera for a shot of the other person listening – or perhaps *not* listening. Then back to camera two to see the first person who's getting agitated – before switching back to the wider shot on camera one to see people at a nearby table taking an interest in the growing argument and so on.

Very little of this needs to be written in the script. It can be suggested at times by writing: 'Pat doesn't react. She just keeps eating.' Or: 'People nearby glance across.' It isn't the writer's job to choose the camera shots (which camera, which lens, how many characters in the frame, etc.). This is the director's job, and he or she (not the writer) will add it to the script at the appropriate time.

As already explained, the script will then be re-typed by a secretary. It will then be photocopied for the director and technicians, and sometimes the actors (who may or may not always need to know exactly where the cameras are pointing).

Make a note	• The writer says *what* we see, not necessarily *how* we see it.

Not telling the actors how to say their lines

If you write a line something like this:

Martin: My best friend. Sleeping with my wife. I could kill you.

There is no need to put '(Angrily)' at the beginning of the line. If you do, the actor delivering the line will either laugh or be insulted. Most actors are clever enough to work out for themselves how a character would be feeling in a situation like this. Only put something explanatory when the meaning is obscure or unexpected, so perhaps:

Martin: (Faintly amused) My best friend. Sleeping with my wife. I could kill you.

This might be appropriate if Martin had actually set up the situation because he was tired of his wife and wanted to get rid of her, and his feelings were now a mixture of triumph and hurt pride. Maybe he had half hoped that neither his friend nor his wife would actually try to deceive him? In this case an actor playing the part *wouldn't* be able to guess how the writer expected this to be portrayed.

In general, avoid giving instructions to the actors as much as you can. Actors are usually very good at understanding how a line should be delivered, which is hardly surprising as this is what they do for a living. They interpret other people's dialogue and bring it to life with suitable expressions of emotion and with actions.

Having said all that, you must take particular care when using irony. If you write something like, 'Had a nice day at work, dear?' 'Yes, terrific,' the person giving the answer must know if it's meant to be genuine or ironic. We may know the person's had a terrible day because we've seen him getting the sack after being caught stealing money from the till so we (and the actor playing the part) would expect it to be ironic. But the character might be saying 'terrific' as if he means it because he doesn't want his wife to start asking questions and find out what's been going on.

In slightly confusing cases like this it would be perfectly reasonable to write either '(Ironically)' or '(Lying)' before the line and nobody would feel insulted. It's all a matter of common sense. You're trying to make things clear to the actors – not patronise them.

Very occasionally, you may write a line that's interrupted. The actor having to say the unfinished line will be unsure how to say it because he or she can't work out where the unfinished line was going. In that case it's perfectly reasonable for you to help the actors by finishing the 'unsaid' part of the dialogue inside brackets, in this manner:

> **John:** Ready?
>
> **Wendy:** What? Oh, but I thought ... (we were staying the night here).
>
> **John:** (A slight warning look) You thought what, dear?
>
> **Wendy:** Oh. Nothing. I didn't realise it was so late ... that's all. (She smiles a bit nervously and reaches for her coat.)

The person playing the part of Wendy will realise that she doesn't have to say the part in brackets but will have no difficulty getting the inflexions right in the fragment she *is* saying. She would also understand that John has changed his mind and probably has reasons for not wanting that to be obvious to the other people present.

Again, there's never any need to do this unless you decide it's necessary to do so. It definitely *wouldn't* be necessary if we had already seen John and Wendy discussing their plans for the evening, but it probably *would* be necessary if this was an early scene. Then there'd be no way for anyone to guess what Wendy was intending to say at this point. So completing the line as shown would be appropriate in these circumstances.

Make a note

- Only add instructions to the actors where the meaning of the line isn't obvious.

Not giving too much detail (characters)

Suppose you describe a character like this: 'Mike is barely five feet tall. He's middle aged, American-Italian, stocky, balding and pugnacious. He talks fast and hard, jabbing a pudgy finger as if shooting the words at people.'

Nothing much wrong with that as a piece of imagery. And if Danny DeVito is available (and affordable) to star in your British sitcom about a police exchange scheme perhaps you could be on to a winner. (Actually it's not that bad an idea when you come to think about it!) But you have severely limited the possibilities for the casting department. Don't do this. Only describe a character in any kind of detail if it's vital to the plot or the idea in general. Most of the time you just need to know if it's a man or a woman, their age and a very brief physical description, if any at all.

Just think how rarely you see an American character appearing in a home-grown TV programme, or a British actor portraying an American. It doesn't happen very often for various reasons, but the excellence of the American film and TV industries means that many of my university students can't resist being influenced by them. I've lost count of the number of times I've read a promising script marred by the fact that it's like a sequel to *The Godfather* but set in somewhere like Skegness or Wolverhampton. As a new writer (and particularly a young one) keep things as easily workable as possible. Leave the risk-taking to seasoned professionals.

So you'd be better to say something like: 'Mike is middle aged, a tough-looking man with the personality of an angry

Rottweiler,' and that would be enough. Apply this rule of simplicity to all your characters. Don't say, 'a stunningly attractive woman of five feet six inches with high cheekbones, jet-black hair, green eyes and a slender waist'; just say, 'an attractive woman of thirty-five', because a woman of five feet three inches with blonde hair, blue eyes and slightly more voluptuous proportions might do just as well.

Make a note

- Describe characters briefly and vividly at first point of entry into the script.
- Don't limit the choice of casting by being too specific.
- Be wary of giving British characters an unconvincing American persona.

Not giving too much detail (things and places)

Suppose that you're really 'into' symbolism and want a particular location to reflect a dispute between neighbours as being something more than a personal thing – perhaps a battle between the forces of good and evil?

Perhaps you decide to set your drama in a rural area of the Midlands and describe in great detail a beautiful farmhouse on the edge of a massive field of ripening corn. You might include a row of pear trees in the lovely farmhouse garden and say that a family of bluetits are twittering away in the topmost branches.

You might then go on to describe a farm nearby with a run-down farmhouse. In this farmhouse garden is a giant oak tree that has been struck by lightning at some time in the past. Its trunk is split almost in two, and half the tree has blackened branches that seem to be reaching out towards the first farmhouse as if to drag it down. On the branches of this tree a line of crows seem to be gazing malevolently towards the 'good' farm. The run-down farm has rusty equipment lying around and an adjoining field has been neglected so badly that it's like a jungle with brambles and stinging nettles leading all the way to a dark and brooding wood.

All of this might be quite effective in the pages of a novel, and visually too it could work on screen. But who is going to search for and find such a location in the area chosen – with the 'right' buildings, plants and animals? Easy enough, perhaps, to find a nice-looking farmhouse with a field of corn (at harvest time) but will there be an adjoining farm that's suitably run-down with a smoke-blackened oak tree? And will there be crows and bluetits readily available to twitter or look malevolent on cue? Yes, all these things could be tackled in a major film production. A tree could be made as a prop and animals could be obtained in one way or another, but in a thirty-minute script aimed at British TV? Forget it.

'An attractive and prosperous farm right next to a run-down one somewhere in the Midlands' would say what you want but leave plenty of scope.

Make a note

- Show common sense when choosing and describing locations.
- Avoid giving details that might be difficult to include.
- Don't expect wild animals to be readily available!

Not giving information the audience won't get

There is no point in describing why a character is behaving in a certain way if this isn't going to be revealed to the audience – especially if you go into great detail. So, 'James, thirty-eight, out of condition and nervous, comes staggering in' is probably enough. You don't have to say that he was abused as a child, that his wife ran off with a door-to-door paraffin salesman shortly after the honeymoon, and that he was so upset he couldn't work and lost his job. Nor that he had his house repossessed and was then told he might have a heart condition made worse by his heavy smoking and drinking.

All this might be useful for you to know when creating the character in the first place, and for story revelations later, but don't write it in the body of the script as if you expect the actor to 'act' it. Some producers like to have brief biographies of the characters, but not mixed up with the actual script. (More about this later.)

Similarly, it's a waste of time and energy describing a place as it used to be before all the half-timbered buildings were knocked down to make way for a multi-storey car park. Just say what we see and get on with it.

Maybe you're old enough to remember some of those classic western films like *Shane* (first shown in 1953)? A man on a horse comes riding into view (and into our lives) and immediately we're interested. We want to know where he's going and what he's going to do when he gets there. We don't need to know where he's coming from or how much he paid for his horse.

Make a note

- Don't write information for the actors that can't be acted.
- Don't describe things that can't be shown on screen.
- Do remember that the viewers can't see your script or read your mind.

Giving Too Much Information

One of the most common failings in a script by a new writer is the desire to give too much information at the beginning. You're afraid the reader won't carry on if you don't show all your skills immediately. This is a big mistake – it just confuses the reader and shows your own anxiety.

You have to display the kind of confidence a successful writer has. He or she knows there's plenty more to come, so they can dole out the information in tasty little chunks – not whopping great spoonfuls. They want the script-reader to think: Aha, this writer knows what he or she is doing. I wonder what happens next?

Make a note

- Don't try to force-feed the script reader with too much information at once.
- 'Less is more' in this instance.
- Show confidence in your ability to keep the reader wanting to find out more.

Common Links: Drama, Sitcom and Soap

The central premise of this book is that you can write one thirty-minute calling-card script to use in four different ways:

1. As a possible one-off drama production. (There are few opportunities for this here at the moment, but things can change.)
2. As a pilot (opening episode) for a new sitcom or drama series that you'll create.
3. As an example of your work to the producer of an existing soap opera.
4. As an example of your work to the producer of an existing drama series.

Most people who dream of writing for TV are usually thinking in terms of one or another of these areas: drama, sitcom or soap – maybe all three – so it's comforting to realise that these three supposedly differing genres have common links. To keep it as simple as possible, let's say they all need:

- at least one character the audience want to follow
- a story with a beginning, middle and end

- a good structure to that story – with effective scene transitions
- an understanding of how TV 'drama' in general works (as opposed to those written for radio, film or stage)
- an awareness of cost.

You can show that you've at least begun to get to grips with these things in virtually *any* drama script.

However, there are some limitations to consider. Firstly, a thirty-minute script written as a sitcom pilot could also be sent to a soap producer or to a drama series producer as an example of your work, but the opposite isn't true. It wouldn't be a good idea to send a thirty-minute script written as a straight drama to the producers of sitcom. There are very few British sitcoms that use a team of writers as, unlike American sitcoms, they tend to be written more or less exclusively by the originators. Teams of writers are usually considered more necessary to fuel soaps that go out several times a week, all year round, and drama series that also have a regular slot. Also, sitcom is generally regarded as more difficult to write. It has everything that drama has, but with something extra. That something extra is of course humour – funny lines, funny situations and funny visuals. A drama with some funny lines isn't a sitcom.

So let me spell it out again. A thirty-minute calling-card script written as a straight drama can be used in four different ways as listed above, but it should *not* be sent to a sitcom producer. A thirty-minute calling-card script written as a sitcom pilot can still be used in four different ways, the only difference being that it will be a pilot for a brand new sitcom instead of a brand new serious drama.

- A script written as sitcom can also be sent to producers of serious drama or soap.
- A script written as straight drama should not be sent to sitcom producers.

I also advise you, as a new writer, not to think in terms of trying to write a pilot episode for a new soap opera. Firstly, the chances of it being considered, let alone accepted, are very slim indeed and, secondly, it's not within the scope of this book.

Creating a new soap opera is much more to do with organising a complicated and risky business venture than creating a single script. It's not the same as creating a new drama or comedy series, where subsequent episodes can be virtual one-offs. It's about continuous storylines with characters who are treated almost as 'real' people living out their everyday lives. Nothing is forgotten and very little is spontaneous. A mountain of planning and detailed record-keeping is required: that means large numbers of people, and that means large sums of money. So, again, leave that to the seasoned professionals (and hope that some day you'll become one of them).

Having said all that, if you have a brilliant idea for a new soap, and won't rest until you've given it a try, by all means go for it. Miracles do sometimes happen. But don't expect to learn all you need to know from this book – or any other that I know of.

Well, these are some of the basics. Before you go on to read Chapter Two, may I suggest you check the listed points. Have you written them in your notepad? Have you highlighted them in the pages of this book? Why not do both? Learn by doing. Learn at a bodily (physical) level – not just by 'thinking' about it.

2 Prepare to be Inspired

One-minute Overview

In this chapter you'll be asked to consider why there is never any shortage of ideas for you to work on. You'll be shown how to look at basic ideas with TV in mind. You'll be given some simple guidelines to help you keep those ideas fresh and exciting but not too expensive or difficult to produce. You'll be given a few of the technical details you need to know before even making a start towards developing an idea into a script.

Where Do Ideas Come From?

Perhaps a better question would be: is there anywhere that ideas don't come from? We live in a cosmic soup of ideas. We are swimming amongst them all the time and we simply can't avoid making contact with them. The minute you accept this you become aware that every single thought you have is inextricably linked to every other thought it's *possible* for you to have. It's not so much a matter of creating thoughts and ideas, as God might create a tree, but of patiently searching until you find the thoughts and ideas you need. (More will be said about generating ideas in Chapter Five)

The most limiting belief you can have is that ideas are somehow stored inside your head like items in a warehouse, stacked in neat rows just waiting to be used, and that when one is used it will be replaced by exactly the same idea (to avoid leaving a gap).

Obviously, if you think like that then you will either be unable to find the idea you want (sorry, we just don't stock that brand) or you will eventually use all the ideas you've got and start to bore your potential customers by offering stuff they've already rejected. That's when you'll hear yourself saying things like, 'I'm really short of ideas on this ...' or, worse: 'I'm sorry. I don't have a single idea in my head.'

Don't do this. Stop looking inside your head and get out more. Start looking around you. Either literally or figuratively. I happen to believe that physical exercise stimulates the brain, and I do a lot of my best thinking on long walks. But you don't have to do that. You can open up your mind to a positive flood of ideas without even getting out of bed these days.

You can read books, watch television, listen to the radio, use the internet, write letters, call people on the phone and so on. There are simply no excuses. Restock those empty shelves with new ideas. The universe is full of them.

So try to see your mind as an exciting workshop rather than a warehouse. Workshops can be vibrant places where raw materials are turned into objects of beauty, but warehouses are often rather cold and unwelcoming places.

Make a note

- There is never any shortage of ideas – the universe is full of them.
- Open up your mind and let them flood in.
- Think of your mind as a workshop, not a warehouse.

Starting Small: Cast, Studio Sets and Locations

You don't need a really 'big' or 'different' idea for your thirty-minute calling-card script. Often the simplest ideas are the most effective, and they are much easier to handle.

Cast

I suggest, as a newcomer, that you limit your cast to something like four to six main characters with perhaps three or four others who may say the odd word.

Obviously that means ten should be the maximum number of speaking characters. It's easy to keep the number of speakers down. Waiters, bar staff, taxi drivers, sales assistants in stores and receptionists in offices rarely need to speak in a drama.

Sometimes their comments *can* be useful and help push the story along, and that's fine – especially if they are going to appear on screen more than once. But never include their comments just to make the script seem more realistic. Yes, in real life all these people are likely to speak, but this isn't real life – it's fiction and it needs to keep moving.

On a purely practical level, performers who speak get paid more than NSEs (non-speaking extras). Always bear this in mind.

Studio sets

This can be quite a tricky thing to calculate. Sometimes a multiple set, like the various rooms of a house, can be counted as *one* set, but don't rely on that and certainly don't expect it to be a ten-roomed house with bedrooms on an upper floor (though sometimes this impression can be given by having cleverly designed segments of a grand house).

It's very unlikely that interior scenes will be shot inside a real house. It's more likely the rooms will be built a bit like stage sets with three walls and an 'invisible' wall, only instead of having an audience in front of the invisible wall there'll be cameras, lighting and sound equipment.

Suppose the multiple set contains the main room of the house, then the kitchen, hall and perhaps one bedroom? These would be attached, but not as they would be in reality – more like a row of cubicles without doors, lined up one against the other or clustered together in a kind of circle with each set facing outwards and all at ground level.

This means that the camera can't always follow the characters if they leave one room to go to another, because in reality they won't be going from one room to another: they'll be moving from one 'set' to another and possibly momentarily stepping into a space between the sets that is part of the warehouse where the sets are standing. So that might require a separate scene to be written every time the action moves from one room to another. Nevertheless, we can probably count that 'multiple set' as one set for purposes of cost at the moment.

I would suggest that you only have another three or four completely separate (and singular) interior locations in addition to this. This might typically be a room in a pub, the inside of a shop, an office or part of a restaurant. Don't imagine that it's easy to film inside 'real' places instead of building studio sets. There might be lots of space for cameras and crew inside a real supermarket, for example, but there will usually also be customers and real trades-people who are trying to get on with their lives. The people who own the supermarket would expect to be paid for closing part of it off and, since many shops now stay open for long hours and for seven days a week, there's little 'spare' time available.

All in all, it's more sensible to assume that any interior scenes you write will be filmed on a studio set and leave it at that. In any case, it's a useful discipline to limit yourself in this way.

Exterior locations

By exterior locations I mean particular spaces where the cameras can be set up to capture specific shots. I don't mean Yorkshire or London to be counted as one location each. I would suggest that you limit yourself to just four or five 'specific' places where the cameras can be set up to film a fairly 'contained' piece of action. These might typically include: a car travelling a short distance along a road, a crowded street, the area immediately outside the main character's house and so on.

One good way to gauge if your choice of exterior locations is reasonable is to try to imagine how difficult it would be for *you* to film it – using actors and technicians to get visuals and dialogue recorded. Professional crew members will of course be more expert than you are at getting the shots they require, but they aren't magicians. They can't clear the streets of people, stop aeroplanes flying overhead, halt the flow of traffic or simply transport themselves and their equipment from one part of a city to another at the speed of light. Try it and you'll see what I mean.

Costume drama

If I say the phrase 'costume drama' to my students they are quite likely to think of men in three-cornered hats and women in crinoline dresses, of ornate palaces in France or the dingy back-street slums of Dickensian London. But in fact this description applies to *any* drama requiring extensive changes to the present norms.

A drama or comedy set just forty or fifty years ago may cause problems because it isn't just the clothing styles that have changed in such a relatively short period. Cars and lorries have changed too, and so have other things we take for granted, like telephone kiosks, TV aerials, children's toys, public buildings, houses and factories – not to mention the ethnic diversity of the population itself. Set your drama at the end of the Second World War or during the beginning of the rock-and-roll era in the fifties and sixties, and you'll create an extra problem to be considered.

Why make difficulties for yourself at this stage in your development? Even though you are writing a calling-card script that's unlikely to be produced, why include *anything* that will give a script-reader a ready excuse to say no?

I think this might be a good place to say something about script-readers in general that most people never really think about. (And here I'm talking about all sorts of script-readers – ones who work for large well-established organisations like the BBC and others who work for the smallest commercial companies and perhaps combine their script-reading with other duties.)

The one thing all of these people have in common is that they are more or less obliged to say 'no' a lot more often than they say 'yes'. The logic behind this is simple: they get a lot of scripts. More than they need or can possibly ever use. Many scripts they receive are so badly written that they can say 'no' to them pretty quickly, and that's probably a relief – they can simply move on to the next one. They are doing their job and getting paid for it.

The minute they spot a script with real potential is when they have a tougher decision to make. Once they recommend it, other busy people will become involved and that can mean a lot of time and money being wasted. They need to be pretty sure about it in the first place. So you see it's likely to be very much easier to say 'no' than 'yes'. A positive decision involves much more risk than a negative one.

Script-readers may be lovely people, but don't make life too easy for them by sending in work they can dismiss in seconds. Keep your calling-card script simple and as free from production difficulties as possible. Don't give them a quick excuse to say 'no' and head for the coffee machine.

Make a note

- Keep your basic idea simple, contemporary and uncluttered.
- Have a maximum of ten speaking characters (four to six main ones).
- Limit your interior sets to an absolute maximum of six including one multiple set (of maybe three rooms).
- Only have four or five exterior locations (and that includes exteriors of main house).

We are still talking about creating ideas here, so perhaps it's enough for you to know at this stage that your calling-card script would be better set in a contemporary and fairly ordinary location than in the past, in a foreign country and dealing with Hannibal and his elephants crossing the Alps. We are talking thirty-minute British TV shows here – not two-hour Hollywood blockbusters.

Inventing the Bicycle

Whilst on the subject of keeping things simple, I must point out that this doesn't mean you'll find it easy. You'll find it easier than you would if you just let your imagination run wild and had twenty speaking characters and locations spread across the globe, but it still won't be easy.

The first efforts you make are likely to be pretty poor. That's understandable and acceptable. Think of the first time you tried to drive a car or swim in a pool or do anything else that takes practice.

One of the wisest things anyone ever said to me about learning to write came from the then Artistic Director at the Derby Playhouse Studio, David Milne. We'd been working together on a comedy play called *Adult Pantomime* and having lots of problems. I'd write a sequence, get it photocopied and present it to the six actors. They'd try to act it out, make suggestions and then throw the discarded pages in the wastebasket. Then I'd go away to do the rewrites and we'd go through the same process again, until at one point David discarded the wastebasket and replaced it with a plastic dustbin.

He saw my look of dismay and asked if he'd put me off. I said not exactly but I'd know it was time to quit when he replaced the dustbin with a skip. The rewrites and the suggestions carried on until finally we had a script that was workable (and eventually quite successful). But the really funny thing was that, having started off with a fairly complex idea, we finally settled on a pretty straightforward script about half the length of the original. I looked at the final script and said to David, 'Why didn't I just write it like this in the first place?' And he said to me, 'For the same reason that the person who invented the penny farthing bicycle didn't invent a multi-speed mountain bike. It just doesn't work like that.'

It was brilliant advice and I've remembered it ever since. You simply can't go from nothing to something special without wading through a lot of junk. So expect to clear the rubbish from your mind before you can produce something good. That's the way it works.

Make a note

- You can't expect to write a final draft on your first go.
- Good writing has to be refined and polished – like gold and diamonds from rocks.

3 Who Says Talk is Cheap (or Easy)?

One-minute Overview

In this chapter you'll be focusing mainly on TV dialogue. You'll learn why dramatic dialogue isn't the same as real-life conversation, and you'll be told about the so-called 'five functions of dialogue'. You'll be shown how important duologues (conversations between two characters) can be in drama, and told something about the dynamics involved. You'll be made aware of some of the dangers to be faced in writing dialogue generally, and shown how visuals can often make dialogue unnecessary.

Creating an Effective Duologue

The exercise you have already done was a duologue (a conversation between two people) but one without much talking. Now we're going to take a closer look at duologues so that I can tell you something really important about TV dialogue. I feel as if some sort of fanfare is needed to introduce this deceptively simple concept because it's so important.

Just notice next time you watch any kind of TV drama how many scenes are predominantly about two people talking together. We may start with two people talking in the corner shop and cut away to two people talking in a house, then we'll go to a crowded pub where two people are talking at a corner table. They'll mention someone who's standing at the bar and we'll join that person, who's having a conversation with the landlord, and so on.

Don't be fooled by the fact that non-speaking characters are also standing around or nodding in agreement – many of these scenes are essentially duologues.

The duologue is at the very heart of drama, soap and sitcom. It's an essential building block. Master that and you'll be like a builder who really knows how to lay bricks to help produce a beautiful building. Imagine what a well-designed house might look like with patches of wobbly and disjointed bricks at various intervals.

Now I think it's time for another writing exercise. The less information I give at this stage the better, so I'll just say: don't try to be clever or 'different', just let the creativity flow in a relaxed manner without too much conscious thought. Don't try to guess what this is leading to and only write a few words for each question. So pick up your pen and pad and write as you follow the guidelines.

Do it now!

1. Write down a person's name in full. (Not a real person – this is fiction we're practising – but don't try to be too clever or 'different', just keep it fairly ordinary.)
2. Write down that person's age and nationality.
3. What is the basic personality type: happy, sad, unpleasant, friendly, sarcastic, jovial, etc?
4. What is the social background: rich, middle class, unemployed, destitute, etc?
5. Where is that person most likely to be found: in a pub, an art gallery, a library, a betting shop etc?

Now repeat the exercise for another fictitious person. Forget what you've just written about the first character. Don't try to match the two characters up or contrast then in any way. Just do it in the same way as you did the first list with no particular end in view. (Or you might like to ask a friend to create a character for you *without* letting that person know anything about the character you've created.)

Do it now!

Now you have two characters ready to engage in a duologue, so think of a suitable venue and let them get on with it. What kind of venue it is depends on what you've already written about these people. Don't worry if they're so different you can't ever see them meeting *anywhere*. That could make it more interesting. A drug-addicted bag lady could easily meet a well-adjusted nursery school teacher in a doctor's surgery, and a famous pop star driving his BMW down a country lane might narrowly avoid hitting a farmer's daughter on a bicycle and then find himself attracted to her quiet, no-nonsense attitude.

Don't think of it as one scene but as a sequence of scenes and, just as with the exercise you did in Chapter One, you don't have to start with them together. We could see them both leaving their respective dwellings and travelling to the meeting spot, by bus, chauffer-driven car, skateboard or whatever, and these scenes could tell us a lot about each character without a word being spoken.

Their meeting could be planned or accidental. It could be friendly or antagonistic. They could be complete strangers or have some connection. Just bear in mind that their conversation should *lead* somewhere and not be meaningless chit-chat. Allow them to take over and grow into 'real' people with minds of their own and see what happens.

Don't try to turn this meeting into a comedy sketch with a definite end. Try to finish with some surprise element that could leave a viewer wondering what's going to happen next. Write for five or ten minutes and then come back to the book. If two of you are doing this exercise, do this part separately, so you can compare your efforts later.

Ready?

Do it now!

I hope you gave it a try. As I've already said, and as I'll carry on suggesting throughout the book, learning by doing is the best and quickest way.

So did you come up with something that excited you? Do you think you could continue this if necessary and turn it into a complete thirty-minute script? Of course you could because, as I said at the beginning of Chapter Two, every thought you have is inextricably linked to every thought it's possible for you to have. Everything in the universe – real or imagined – is connected to everything else. All you have to do is find interesting ways of making these connections. Two people meet and the possibilities of a story growing from this meeting are infinite.

Now here are a couple of questions to ask yourself regarding the duologue you've just written. Did both characters seem like 'real' people with their own personalities? Did they both have an interest in the dialogue or was one character doing all the talking and the other just there to provide a listener?

Sometimes this is fine in the context of a real script when we are 'following' the activities of the main character and aren't really bothered what the second character feels, but whilst we're practising it's a good idea to write something where both characters are involved and have an agenda. This makes the scene more difficult to write but usually more interesting too. And of course it's good practice for later on when you'll be attempting scenes with three or more characters, all interacting at the same time.

Whose Scene Is It?

Another interesting thing about duologues is that you usually find that one character is 'driving' the scene and the other is playing a secondary role. The writer does this without really thinking, because he or she will automatically identify with one character and see things through that person's eyes. You can easily change the dynamics of the duologue by switching these primary and secondary roles.

Suppose, for example, we have a duologue where a young girl is telling her mother she's pregnant. The scene will either be recognisably the scene where the girl *tells* her mother she's pregnant, or, paradoxically, the scene where the mother *hears* that her daughter is pregnant. We, the audience, will know which way around this is because we'll know which character is the pivotal one at that point. We'll know because we will tend to 'stay' with that pivotal character throughout the exchange.

We will probably be with them before the exchange begins and after it ends. It can sometimes be disconcerting if the focus of the story switches from one character to another, and occasionally when a scene doesn't seem to be flowing this can be the cause of the problem – an inadvertent switch in focus. The viewer is led into the duologue thinking they were supposed to be empathising with one character – only to see that character disappear and the other one getting all the attention.

Just give that a moment's thought. Did this happen in your duologue? Did you come in with your attention firmly fixed on one character and end with it on the other? Or did you attempt to see the exchange through the eyes of both characters at the same time? This can work – especially in a soap where there are lots of characters of a similar dramatic 'weight' to consider – but even in these cases you'll usually find the focus stays on one person throughout a particular exchange before picking up the 'story' of the other one.

Different Voices

Did each character speak with their own voice or could their sentences have been switched from one character to the other without much difficulty? (Here I'm not talking about the content of what they're saying but about their speech patterns and delivery.) If you read the lines aloud (and you really must) then you should get a clear feeling that there's a recognisable difference in the way each character speaks.

Lots of people do of course have similar ways of talking, and you can't *always* differentiate between every single one of them, but we are dealing with just two people here so it shouldn't be a problem. Watch and listen closely to the people you meet in the future – see what you can learn about this fascinating subject and try to use it in your writing.

You'll find, for instance, that some people speak softly and hesitantly and choose their words carefully and others blurt things out and then constantly correct themselves. You'll see that some people talk almost exclusively in clichés, saying things like 'At the end of the day', 'Twenty-four-seven', 'In this day and age' and by adding 'You know?' after almost every sentence. Then there are others who talk as if they are giving a lecture and say things like, 'I feel at this juncture it's incumbent upon me to point out the error in some of your assertions.'

Make a note

- Good dialogue should be written specifically for each character.
- It should not be interchangeable.

Writing Dialect

You have to be very cautious here because a script littered with phonetically spelled words can be extremely tedious to read. I happen to come from Derby, where people have an accent that's not as easy to recognise as some others and which is quite difficult to write phonetically.

For example, you might have a man from Derbyshire saying something like, 'Eyup, mi' duck, wher' art thi goin?' I suppose most actors could recognise this as being, 'Hello, my dear, where are you going?' and have a good stab at saying it 'in character'. But Derbyshire people also say any word with the soft 'u' sound in a kind of guttural grunt – bucket, bus, and so on – that can't really be written. Many also say 'goo-in' rather than 'going' but to write this kind of thing rather than letting the actors get a feel for it seems excessive.

I'm sure the same difficulties exist with other dialects, 'Brummie' (Birmingham) being a good example, where the rhythm of the sentences effects the speech as much as the pronunciation of individual words. And how could you write that?

So, to avoid writing pages of lines that will tax a reader's patience, I suggest you start by specifying that a character talks with a certain accent and then write the lines, paying more attention to the speech patterns than the individual words. Give just some of the words an easily recognised phonetic spelling without making the whole script look as if it's written in hieroglyphics.

And please bear in mind that even the most polished and 'correct' speakers rarely say 'it is,' 'you are' or 'they are' and so on. They nearly always use contractions: 'it's' 'you're' and 'they're'. And you must get into the habit of writing your dialogue like that.

Before you spend too much time checking your duologue against the advice given above, let's take a look at a duologue of my own. This is an excerpt from a sitcom pilot

I sold first to Thames TV and later to the BBC (after Thames had agreed to release their rights to it), but which still hasn't made it to the screen.

It's something I'm quite proud of and based (very loosely, I hasten to add) on events leading up to the death of my father. The action is supposed to take place in and around Derby and the characters would speak accordingly, but as you'll see, there are few odd spellings. I just didn't think it was necessary.

A teacher, one of the main characters, and based on myself, is sitting by the bedside of his dying father. The teacher's brother has just said his goodbyes before leaving for a short while. I'm going to reproduce this excerpt in something more like a recognised TV format, but don't worry about the look of it. I'll be saying more about that later. Just read it first and then study the content after reading my comments that follow:

13. INT. HOSPITAL. EVENING

[JAMES IS MARKING EXERCISE BOOKS AS HE LEANS ON THE BED. SAM IS STILL LYING IN SILENCE.]

JAMES: (TO SAM BUT ABSENTLY) You should be proud of me, Dad. Listen to this from a ten year old ... (HE READS FROM BOOK HE'S MARKING) The blossom twisted and twirled in the air like a troupe of fairy ballerinas and covered the grass like a velvet carpet ... (TO SAM) See what I mean? (READING AGAIN) Then our dog, Brandy, came running out of the house and dumped a great big pile of ... (HE STOPS IN DISGUST) Huh ... That would have been a gold star. (HE REACHES FOR HIS LITTLE TOBACCO TIN OF STARS AND PULLS TO OPEN IT. IT OPENS WITH A JERK AND FLIES

FROM HIS HAND, SCATTERING LITTLE STARS, SOME RED, SOME GOLD, ALL OVER SAM'S FACE. THE OLD MAN WAKES UP.)

SAM: Eh ... What's this? Confetti?

JAMES: No. I was just ... (SHOWS BOOK) stars ...

SAM: Thank God for that ... A funeral I can just about manage, but another marriage ... that'd kill me. (HE TRIES TO LAUGH BUT COUGHS AND WHEEZES)

JAMES: You've just missed Eddie and the others.

SAM: (SMILING TO PROVE JAMES WRONG) Aye, nearly ... not a bad epitaph, was it?

JAMES: Epitaph? Dad. What are you talking about?

SAM: James ... I worry about you sometimes ... and Kate.

JAMES: Why?

SAM: Never doing anything wild or exciting. Tell you what ... sell my house, right now, and blow the lot on a trip to Hawaii ... will you do that for me?

JAMES: I can't.

SAM: I knew it.

JAMES: No, Dad. Really, I can't ... because you live in a council house and you're three months behind with the rent.

SAM: (FUMBLING WITH SCRAP OF PAPER FROM UNDER PILLOW) Here.

JAMES: What is it?

SAM: Hymns, for my send-off.

JAMES: (READING) Ding Dong Merrily On High? (NO RESPONSE) I ... Oh. Fair enough, Dad ... If that's what you want.

SAM: Promise?

JAMES: Yeah, promise.

SAM: Good lad ... Oh, and one more thing ... You always thought I favoured Eddie, didn't you?

JAMES: Well ...

SAM: I didn't ... you, Eddie, Teresa, Walter, Eric, Henry and Ann. I loved you all the same and I want you to know that.

JAMES: Thanks Dad. I'm glad you told me, except ... who are Teresa, Walter, Eric and ... erm ... that other one?

SAM: Eh ... what?

JAMES: No, nothing, it doesn't matter now.

SAM: Do you think she'll be there ... waiting for me?

JAMES: Who?

SAM: Who? Your mother of course.

JAMES: She always was.

SAM: And she was the only one ... really.

JAMES: Yeah, course she was.

SAM: Goodbye, son.

JAMES: No, Dad, not goodbye ... so long, like Eddie said. Oh, and Dad ... we did love you – me, Eddie and all those others ... not all the time perhaps, but most of it, and that can't be bad, can it? Dad, Dad, my team, we're going to be in the final ... that's great, isn't it? Dad, don't ...

[BUT THE OLD MAN IS NOW PERFECTLY STILL. JAMES VERY GENTLY TAKES A GOLD STAR FROM SAM'S HAIR.]

JAMES: See, this is a gold one. (HE PICKS UP THE EXERCISE BOOK HE'D BEEN MARKING AND STAMPS THE GOLD STAR IN IT.) How's that for being wild? Eh, Dad? (THEN HE DROPS HIS HEAD TO SHED A TEAR.)

As I said, this was based very loosely on the last visit I paid to my own father in hospital. He really did give me a list of the hymns he wanted at his funeral and he really was very brave and made jokes about the situation, but those are about the only bits that were true. My mother was still alive at the time and my father had never been a rogue, told lies or failed to pay his bills. I just used him as a starting point to create a larger-than-life sitcom character.

I've chosen to use this particular excerpt because I think it shows that sitcom can be funny without being silly. It can have depth as well as humour, and in my opinion is all the stronger for doing so.

I also chose it to demonstrate what some teachers of scriptwriting call:

The Five Functions of Dramatic Dialogue

Let's make one thing very clear. TV dialogue can and perhaps should sound more realistic than either stage dialogue or radio dialogue, and there'll be slightly more of it than you'd get in a feature film, but it isn't real speech. It should be shorter, snappier and more interesting than real speech.

Unlike real speech, which is generally chaotic and discursive (however interesting), and which changes constantly depending on who the speaker happens to meet, dramatic dialogue has certain specific functions to perform. These can be listed as follows:

Dramatic dialogue either for TV, radio, stage or film must strive to:

1. Push the story along.
2. Give necessary information.
3. Delineate character.
4. Have a subtext.
5. Set up or pay off a funny line.

Most of the things in this list are self explanatory, but just to make sure you're not in any doubts let me give a bit more detail and use my script excerpt as an example.

Push the story along

A thirty-minute TV piece needs pace. There's no time to do leisurely introductions of characters or situations. Something should be 'happening' or just about to happen. It may be something to do with the main story or something to do with a secondary story (or sub-plot) but it can't stand still.

Note that in the excerpt from my script someone dies. This is obviously a very serious and potentially powerful happening but there is still the promise of other stories developing with Sam's warning about the state of James's marriage and his mention of James being a bit jealous of his brother Eddie – also his mention of other children that James knows nothing about. Could there be trouble at the funeral, for example, and will James be taking a closer look at his marriage partner?

Give necessary information

A lot of background information is given about James, his father and the family situation in general. We can see that James is a decent and hard-working teacher but that he may be about to experience some difficulties in his marriage. We can see that Sam has had a colourful life and was probably seen as a likeable rogue.

Delineate character

Both characters manage to say more about themselves than they intend, so the dialogue is relevant to them as individuals. Nobody has to say out loud that Sam is brave. We can see it. Nobody has to say that Sam was a bit of a lad. We can see it. Nobody has to say that James might be paying too much attention to his job at the expense of other people. He's marking work at his father's deathbed – even if he is managing to do it without seeming callous or uncaring about his father.

Have a subtext

Subtext is what the characters are giving away – without actually saying it. This has already been covered in the remarks above about character delineation but it can have a wider context too – giving clues about possible developments as well as personalities. Subtext is what enables us to glean information about people and situations other than what is obvious. It is often the writer telling us, either consciously or subconsciously, what the story is really about.

Subtext is about the theme rather than the action. If the story tells us *what* happens – then the theme tells us *why* it happens (or, more correctly, why the writer chose to tell it this way).

Dialogue can only have subtext if there's some depth to the characters in the first place.

Set up or pay off a funny line

This is the one rule out of the five that doesn't always apply. Although 'good' dialogue should always have traces of the first four rules (or at least *some* of them) it's perfectly possibly to write excellent dialogue without a trace of humour. Having said that, even the most lurid murder mystery can sometimes benefit from the occasional witty remark. As for the dialogue in my own excerpt, you'll have to judge for yourself if I managed to make it funny. Certainly that was my intention – to make it funny but poignant at the same time.

You probably know all about these functions of dialogue already, even if only at a subconscious level, but it's very useful to state them clearly so that you'll be in no doubt whatsoever. Naturally, you won't sit down to write with these things at the forefront of your mind. You won't think: I'm going to start off with a bit of character delineation and then sneak in some necessary information with just a dash of subtext, and then throw in a few belly laughs to round it all off. No, you don't work like that at all. You simply write the scene or sequence as you see it unfolding and then use the five functions *afterwards* as a checklist.

You'll then also check to see if you can make it more interesting visually, but don't worry about that at the moment – we'll go into that in more detail later. For the time being we are concentrating on dialogue.

Why don't you stop at the end of this paragraph and check your own duologue against the five functions? In fact, don't just check. Rewrite – adding anything you think it needs (but not humour if it's inappropriate or doesn't come naturally to you). Take as much or as little time as you like to do this, but I'd suggest anything from ten to twenty minutes. You can always go back to it later.

Do it now!

I hope you found doing this both useful and illuminating. I know I always do. Using these functions as a checklist allows you to avoid writing what the American guru of scriptwriting Robert McKee terms in his workshop sessions 'on-the-nose dialogue'. That is, dialogue that states the perfectly obvious, or waffles on to no effect whatsoever.

Don't Use Unnecessary Dialogue

Let me give a brief example of this. Suppose two people, say Alan and his wife Hilary, are sitting in their living room and the doorbell rings. Hilary looks at Alan and says, 'Was that the doorbell?' Alan says, 'Yes. I wonder who it can be at this time on a Saturday morning?'

Hilary says, 'Will you answer it, dear, or shall I?' Alan says, 'I'll get it,' and heads for the door. He opens the door to find an older woman standing there. Alan smiles. 'Hello, Sarah,' he says. The woman (Sarah) also smiles and says, 'Hello, Alan. I was just passing and decided to call in. I hope you don't mind.' Alan says, 'Of course not. It's good to see you. Come in.' Sarah comes in and Alan shouts to Hilary, 'Look Hilary. It's Sarah. She was just passing and decided to call in.' 'Hello, Sarah' says Hilary. 'Hello, Hilary,' says Sarah.

And on and on it goes with Sarah being asked if she'd like a cup of tea and how bad the traffic was, and after just a minute or so of this wouldn't you be throwing things at the screen and screaming 'For heaven's sake get on with it'?

You know instinctively that this isn't good dramatic dialogue. It's repetitive, it isn't going anywhere and it isn't 'doing' anything. It's 'real' speech, and unless these people are relatives of yours you are not involved.

Now imagine the same scene again but this time giving more consideration to the audience. Alan and his wife Hilary are relaxing in their living room scanning the papers. The radio plays classical music softly. The doorbell rings. Hilary looks at Alan and groans. 'Oh no ... not every weekend ... please God ...'

Alan tries to be positive and says, 'It could be anybody (pause and change of expression) but just in case ... we won't answer it.' They sit in a tense silence for a few seconds. Then the doorbell rings again. Hilary says, 'The radio.' Alan shushes her, 'I can hardly hear it myself and she's nearly seventy.'

Hilary remembers something else and groans, 'The bedroom windows are wide open.' Alan looks at her and says, 'The drainpipe's made of plastic. It'll never take her weight.' Hilary sighs and says, 'Let her in before she gives it a try.' The doorbell rings again and then a voice is heard shouting through the letterbox. 'Alan. You probably can't hear me because of the radio.' Alan and Hilary just look at each other with raised eyebrows.

In this reworking there's less dialogue but much more is said. Now, we haven't even seen the third character and we're not sure who she is. She could be the mother of either of them, a nosy neighbour or an eccentric aunt, but we know she's not exactly welcome and there's a promise of some conflict to come – even if it's only light-hearted sitcom stuff.

It could of course have been played with deadly seriousness. This could be a debt collector, an unwelcome suitor for their daughter, or a neighbour from hell they're dreading. And still we could start it off with no waffle and little action. Remember what I said earlier about less usually being more on television.

Could you really apply the five functions of dialogue to a tiny snippet like this and get a result? Why not try it and see? And, as always, check for visuals – facial expressions or whatever – that could make even some of this fairly 'tight' dialogue unnecessary.

Make a note

- Always let your writing flow at first.
- Only use the five functions of dialogue as a checklist later.
- Check every scene for simple visuals as well.
- Avoid on-the-nose dialogue.

Using Swear Words

If your script is definitely going to be used as a 'calling card' aimed at getting you work on a soap or series then you'll know that most of these shows go out before what's called the watershed (the time after which younger children shouldn't be watching). They don't usually use swear words, and I suggest that your script follows suit.

If you are writing a script that you hope might actually be produced then you must make your own decisions. I personally don't welcome the increasing use of swear words on screen. I don't see it only as a matter of morality and taste but of laziness too. It's so easy to write one swear word after another instead of thinking up more interesting ways of saying things.

I tell my students how Shakespeare would have a character come on stage and say something like, 'Light thickens, the crow makes wing to rooky wood, Good things of day begin to droop and drowse, And night's black agents to their preys do rouse.'

I then ask them how that might be written today by one of our modern young writers who are so determined to 'push the barriers' and make drama more 'realistic' and suggest: 'It's getting effing dark.' I then ask them how many teachers of creative writing they think will be quoting such lines in 400 years' time.

I'm not advising you to write in blank verse or use mock-Elizabethan phrases – or even to be too 'wordy' in general – just not to go too far in the other direction either. Think about it.

4 Getting in Shape

One-minute Overview

In this chapter you'll be reminded of how important it is to stay focused. You'll be told about the basic TV story shape and how using it as a guide will ensure you don't go off course and lose the interest of your reader (and eventually viewer) in the process. Each component of this basic story shape will be explained in clear but brief detail.

The Importance of the Pivotal (or Viewpoint) Character

We've already talked about individual scenes in a drama or comedy having a pivotal character, so you probably won't be surprised to learn that the whole story usually has a pivotal character too. This is the main reason why people watch these shows – to see what happens to the central character. They don't watch them out of general interest in the way they might watch a documentary or a circus.

Take an obvious example, like the James Bond films. Without the central character for us to follow and care about, these films would be nothing more than a series of spectacular incidents. There'd be no story.

Sometimes it's perfectly obvious who the pivotal character is, and at other times two or more central characters seem to share the focus. Soaps, dramas and sitcoms can differ in this respect because soaps and serial dramas will be running several storylines at the same time, each centred around a different character, whereas a sitcom may very well have the same central character each time.

It's important for you, as the writer, not to lose focus and confuse the audience, so be very clear who your pivotal character is and stick with that person from start to finish. Remember, this is a one-off script you're writing, not an episode from a soap.

You can have a secondary character who is also important but not *quite* as important as your central character. We *start* with the central character's story and *finish* with it. Everyone else's story begins and ends somewhere in between. And, just as with the duologue we discussed earlier, a change of pivotal character can alter the shape of a story completely – even if you have the main characters engaged in the same dilemma.

One of the exercises my students really enjoy is where we explore the changes that occur with a viewpoint switch. I might describe a simple scenario that includes three characters, such as a married couple and one of their closest friends. I will then split the class into three groups. One group will write a one-page outline for a script using the married man as the pivotal character – another group will have the married woman as the pivotal character and the remaining group will write it from the friend's point of view.

Perhaps you'd like to try a simplified version of this exercise with a couple of friends who are interested in writing? If not you can do the whole thing yourself. It shouldn't take more than fifteen minutes from start to finish. You're just going to scribble down a few opening ideas that point you in a certain direction.

You don't need to write a complete story outline, as my students do, at this stage. Just a few paragraphs to give you the general idea should be enough to get the point across. Five minutes or so on each story will be plenty – and you'll learn a lot. If you want to spend longer on it that's fine, but probably no longer than fifteen minutes on each version or you'll get stuck on that one and be reluctant to have a go at a differing one.

Here is the basic situation:

Craig and Emma Middleton are a married couple in their late thirties who seem to be doing very well. They have good jobs, share a lovely home and have plenty of money to spend. But there's a snag. Emma feels that her biological clock is running down and she desperately wants a baby. Craig 'seems' to be sympathetic and open to having a family but Emma still doesn't get pregnant. They have a mutual friend who just happens to be a doctor. He (or she) becomes involved and that's when things start to go badly wrong.

I want you to think about this situation in general for a few moments and then decide which character you see as the pivotal character.

Once you've decided on your pivotal character I'd like you to write down a few ideas about what story ideas might flow from it. It's not necessary to come up with a complete storyline at this stage – we'll be doing that kind of thing a bit later. So for the moment just get a feel for the basic possibilities.

Then either come back to the book or complete the full exercise by doing it twice with each of the other characters taking the lead. Don't be afraid to make mistakes. This is still just practice and you'll be using your mistakes as stepping-stones to get where you want to be.

Do it now!

Welcome back, and let me give you a few very brief examples of how it might have gone:

With Emma as pivotal character

Emma is frustrated by her continuing failure to get pregnant. She approaches Simon, the doctor friend, and asks him to impregnate her with sperm from a suitable donor. Simon refuses and strongly advises Emma to do nothing before discussing it with her husband. But Emma makes her own arrangements without medical help. When she tells Craig she is pregnant he is stunned. He has been keeping a secret from Emma. He's had a vasectomy and knows the baby can't be his. Simon knew this too but couldn't tell Emma.

You can see how this could develop. Craig might give his wife an ultimatum – either have a termination or ruin the marriage. This would be even more dramatic if Emma is not only desperate to have a baby but also fervently anti-abortion. And maybe Emma is just as angry with Craig for deceiving her, by keeping his vasectomy a secret in the first place.

So what will she decide to do? Will she leave Craig and go it alone? Will she have the abortion but be unable to cope with what she's done and end up completely on her own? Will she perhaps find true love with the more sympathetic (and honest) Simon? Perhaps, but if it ends in tragedy, with the focus still on Emma, the theme would probably be a cautionary one about 'reaping what you sow'.

With Craig as pivotal character

Craig is struggling to expand the business he owns and has never been so glad that Emma earns a large salary of her own. That's when Emma tells him she's pregnant. Craig is shocked. He knows the baby can't be his. He's had a vasectomy. He actually suspects that their doctor friend Simon might be the father until Emma tells him the truth. She's used the services of some dodgy company advertising on the internet.

Craig says that if Emma agrees to an immediate abortion he will promise to have the vasectomy reversed at a later date – when his business is back on course. But Emma is anti-abortion and is furious with Craig anyway. She can't do it. This leaves Craig to decide between saving his marriage or his business – or perhaps trying to work out a way to do both. Craig might then come to realise he cares more for his wife than his business and support her over the baby. He might sell off his business and re-invest in something smaller that both he and Emma can be excited about.

The theme could now be one of 'triumph over adversity' as the baby, the business, the friendships with the doctor and the marriage all survive.

And for a *really* unlikely twist at the end it might turn out that the baby is Craig's anyway. If the vasectomy had reversed itself (which can happen), Emma could already have been pregnant before having the sperm donation. Admittedly this is a bit of a 'sitcommy' ending, but who said it couldn't be?

Although the basics are the same as before, when we had Emma as the pivotal character, now there are obvious differences in tone and storyline. For a greater contrast let's look at what might happen with the doctor as pivotal character.

With the doctor as pivotal character

Simon is a GP but neither Emma nor Craig are patients of his. He is approached by Emma for advice on becoming pregnant, without her husband's knowledge. It now transpires that Simon has always been in love with Emma and jealous of Craig. He is suddenly aware of the possibilities now open to him. He secretly uses his own sperm to impregnate her.

It turns out that Simon has always known about Craig's vasectomy and is hoping the marriage will break up once

Craig hears about the pregnancy. He, Simon, will be there to pick up the pieces. He can decide later if he will ever tell Emma that he's the real father of her child (without, of course, admitting that he knew about Craig's vasectomy).

However, to let Simon get away with this would probably be a mistake – alienating a large percentage of the audience – so something must go wrong. Probably Craig will find out about Simon's involvement and all will be revealed. It might be a happy ending of sorts for Emma and Craig but not for Simon, whose career and perhaps life will be ruined.

Again, the theme would be to do with 'reaping what you sow' but in this case it would also be about corruption and 'the dangers of succumbing to temptation'.

Or, keeping Simon as the pivotal character, we might widen the whole thing to encompass global problems – the issue of single mothers in poor circumstances being forced to 'sell' their babies, for instance. This could easily lead to Simon being blackmailed by criminals involved in the trafficking of babies. Maybe they'd want him to supply fertility drugs. His initial act of compassion could spiral into a nightmare, and the theme this time could deal with larger issues of morality and politics.

Now you see how easy it can be to go from sitcom to deadly serious drama, still using the same basic ingredients but just changing the pivotal character.

Make a note

- Change the pivotal character and you change the focus.
- This can influence storyline, tone and theme.
- Always pay attention to whose story it is.
- Have a strong storyline but also some deeper meaning to it all.
- Remember, the story is *what* happens and the theme is *why* it happens.

The Basic TV Story Shape

Perhaps, after talking so much about pivotal characters and giving examples of the differing ideas these can suggest, this is as good a place as any to talk about what may be described as the basic TV story shape. It goes something like this:

1. Introduce main character/s and set tone and general location.
2. Provide hook.
3. Complications.
4. Climax.
5. Resolution.

This five-step sequence is merely an adaptation of the 'classic' story shape in general – with the smallest of changes to steps one and two, which are particularly important in TV dramas. All sorts of stories fit into this shape, from the simplest of fairy stories to the most complex of novels and screenplays.

To some degree we all understand this at a subconscious level, even as small children. We know that a good story is more than a series of incidents, however interesting, that simply happen for no particular reason or purpose.

We know that a story is *about* something. We usually 'follow' someone we care about, or at least are interested in, who has a desire to achieve something. The story begins with the recognition of that desire and ends when the desire is over, when the person has either achieved their goal or given up on it – either because they realise it wasn't worth having in the first place, or because they've actually *achieved* it (or something better).

Or perhaps the story ends when the pivotal character is content with having made the effort and failed, knowing that in life the greatest risk of all is to risk nothing. Which, of course, also applies very strongly to you as a would-be writer.

Why a strong opening is vital

As already stated, a TV drama or comedy usually starts with a main character and a task to be undertaken or a problem to be solved. That takes care of the first two steps in the list above. We've met the main character or characters, been given the general location and tone and recognised the 'hook' (the task or problem to be faced), which leaves us wanting to know more.

In the case of a thirty-minute TV script all these things should be stated clearly and quickly – within the first two or three pages. In fact, ideally, we should meet the main character or characters on the first page and get the 'hook' more or less straight away – certainly before page three.

There is a very good reason for this and for why it applies particularly to TV and radio scripts rather than to film scripts, stage plays or novels. People *pay* to go into cinemas and theatres after maybe standing in a queue to get their tickets. They are not going to get up and leave after a few minutes – or even at all. No matter how terrible the film or play turns out to be they will probably stick it out to the bitter end (a bit illogical really, wanting to punish yourself further because you've *paid* for it, but there it is – human beings can be strange creatures, which is what makes writing about them so interesting). People are also often prepared to carry on reading a book that's slow to get started, but with television and radio it's different. It's so easy to reach for the controls and search for another programme or simply switch off and take the dog for a walk. Ordinary viewers and listeners know all this, so the people who work in the industry will understand it even better.

As a new writer you need to be aware that if the first two or three pages in your script don't make an impact but it's brilliant *after* that, nobody will ever know. The person reading your script just won't get to the exciting bits. They will have lost interest and given up. You will have wasted your own time and everybody else's.

So don't do that – start with a bang. There's an old story about a famous Hollywood producer who is supposed to have said to a writer: 'I want this film to start with an earthquake and then build up to an exciting climax.' That was probably a joke, so don't take it too literally, but it certainly gets the point across. (More will be said about effective openings in a later chapter.)

The complications

If the task is accomplished or the problem solved straight away then it's not a very satisfying story, which is where the complications come in. Complications can occur when the pivotal character finds another obstacle to surmount or when a sub-plot is introduced (and then both main plot and sub-plot can meet further complications).

The complications form the main part of the whole thing. It's usually better if, after the initial 'bang', the complications start small and then build as the stakes are raised, leading – eventually – to an exciting climax.

The climax

This is obviously the dramatic high-spot of the drama. The point at which the main risk is faced and overcome. Often, to increase the tension, there will be a slight pause after some hiccup in the flow of events.

The main character is approaching the climax and we think all is going well – until suddenly it's revealed that the gun in his hand isn't loaded, or the back up he or she was expecting hasn't arrived. Then the main character has to face whatever problem there is with raw courage and perhaps ingenuity. This pause before the final test is a bit like the tense moment at the start of a race, when the athletes are poised like coiled springs after being told 'On your marks', and then have to wait for the starting pistol.

The resolution

This is the shortest part of the script and can last just a few seconds. It's the bit where the hero kisses the heroine, accepts the Oscar or rides away into the distance looking for the next adventure.

And that's it really. The basic story shape.

The story shape as a whole

Sometimes it's helpful to see the whole process as a circular movement rather than a linear one. If a story proceeds in linear fashion then things just keep happening one after another with little discernible progress because there's no end in sight. Instead of a story we then have a series of incidents that eventually come to a stop in the middle of nowhere.

So it can help to visualise it as a simple diagram – a circular timer like a clock face but with numbers going from nought to thirty instead of nought to sixty, and marked off individually. Within the first minute the main character or characters should be introduced. Between that point and the third minute the hook should have been stated. The complications start and escalate as we get towards the halfway point (fifteen minutes) and a little way beyond it.

Then things seem to improve as the main characters begin to feel more determined and start on the upward curve.

By roughly the three-quarter mark (say twenty-two minutes) they think they are about to succeed and complete whatever they have to do, but a few minutes later they have a real crisis. Suddenly it seems that all is lost. With just six minutes to go (at point twenty-four) they have to renew their determination and decide to carry on, even though defeat now looks like a real possibility. That moment of crisis brings them to the 'do or die' moment that is the climax.

The climax is resolved in the next five minutes, leaving us with just one more minute to round it all off with a meaningful resolution, as already explained.

This is of course only a rough guide, and many successful stories, TV dramas and films won't follow it *at all*, but it's better to have some sort of plan than none at all. And this basic shape really can help. You start with the main characters and a problem or task. You let them travel in a circular route and you end up right back where you started, except with the main character, and the audience, feeling differently.

As I said earlier, even children understand that this is how a good story works. Right at the beginning you know what the end is going to be. The main character or characters get what they want and then the story is over. What keeps you interested is the fact that you don't know *how* it's going to be done.

As writing guru Robert McKee stated in one of his workshops, right near the beginning of the film *Jaws* we know that the sheriff will kill the shark and that will be the end of the film. But imagine if you had watched the start of this film, following the complications leading up to the most critical moment, until just as the sheriff and his helpers are setting out on their final attempt to kill the shark they are approached by some fishermen in another boat who shout, 'Guess what, you guys? We've just killed a great big shark.'

How would you feel if the music played and a caption appeared on the screen saying 'The End'? You wouldn't believe it. You wouldn't want to leave your seat in the cinema and go home.

Make a note

- A story is more than a collection of incidents.
- Think of a story as being circular, rather than linear.
- With a good story the audience often know what the ending will be. They just don't know *how* it's going to be achieved.

5 Let's Get Busy

One-minute Overview

In this chapter you will learn more about creating basic ideas. You'll then be encouraged to try your hand at writing an opening sequence and a more complex scene (one involving more than two speaking characters). You'll be told why it's important to give your main characters a brief biography and how this can help the story develop convincingly. You'll be told how the storyline can build momentum by raising the stakes. You'll learn the difference between 'theme' and 'storyline'. You'll be shown how to analyse a suitable TV drama and learn from it, and you'll be reminded about the need to keep the production costs within reason.

Create a One-page Story Idea in Minutes

We are really talking about a story *outline* here, not a complete story with all the trimmings. This will be something you can eventually turn into a thirty-minute TV script. You'll hear it said by some people in the business that, if you can't say what your idea is about in a few sentences, you haven't really got an idea.

I'm not so sure this is true, because not everyone is good at distilling a complicated idea into a few neat phrases. But it's another skill you can learn, and a useful one too, because TV producers and script-editors are busy people and any time you get to spend with them is almost certainly going to be limited.

Obviously the faster you can get your point across the better, but sometimes the real selling-point is in the details, not the basic idea. So I'd say don't worry too much if you can't get it down to a few paragraphs. In any case we are talking here about an outline for your own use (in the early days, before you become a professional scriptwriter) not necessarily something to be shown to anyone else. It's a wonderful starting point to know that you have an idea that's going somewhere, and that it does have a beginning, a middle and an end.

Please take it that I'm using the phrase 'one page' as a gross simplification. It might be more accurate (but less satisfying as an image) to describe it in terms of word count, say 400 to 750 words.

Remember what I said earlier about ideas being everywhere? They're not merely to be found nestling quietly inside your head but happening all the time around you, just waiting to be noticed. If you've been doing the exercises you've already had experience of two simple ways of generating ideas: simply starting with a few random bits of dialogue and seeing where that leads, or thinking of two characters and putting them into a situation where they have to interact.

Now I'm going to tell you of a few other, slightly more elaborate methods, that I regularly use to generate ideas that can lead to complete stories.

The interrupted routine

This is another thing I learned from the pages of Keith Johnstone's excellent book *Impro*. Keith says that a writer doesn't have to start off by thinking how to make up a story – something that can be very daunting – but can simply start by interrupting a routine and seeing where that leads.

So, to give a few examples off the top of my head: a woman goes into town to buy a new dress. If she simply finds a dress she likes and buys it, that's not a story, it's a description of an ordinary routine. But suppose she's in a cubicle trying on a dress, hears an argument taking place, peeps out through a gap in the curtain and sees an assistant being stabbed to death? Perhaps she gets a good look at the murderer before he or she runs out of the shop, and perhaps the murderer sees her too and thinks about the implications of this before being scared off by another customer entering the shop?

This is still not a story, but it's certainly something that could develop into one. The routine has been well and truly interrupted and we are interested in knowing what might happen next.

On a lighter note, my wife was once trying on dresses in a shop when she suddenly realised she was going to be late to pick up the children from school. She panicked, pulled on her coat, thrust the dresses she'd chosen back onto the rail, rushed out of the shop and onto a bus that was just pulling away.

It wasn't until she had paid her fare and sat down that she realised she was only wearing her knickers and bra under her coat. She had left her own dress on the rail with all the others. This was embarrassing enough, but suppose she hadn't fastened her coat properly and it had blown open just as she joined the regular crowd of parents waiting at the school playground? Or if, instead of leaving her own dress behind, she had rushed out still wearing one of the dresses belonging to the shop and had been arrested for shoplifting?

Any routine can be interrupted in similar fashion. A man's been doing the same boring but secure job every day of his life and is suddenly made redundant. Will his life crumble or will he find the courage to pursue something he'd always wanted to do but thought too risky?

A woman has devoted most of her life to her children and is looking forward to the day when they're grown up and she can spend more time with her husband, who is soon to take early retirement. But that's precisely when her widowed mother has a stroke and needs round-the-clock care. What's the woman going to do now – put her mother in a care home and live with the guilt? Or take her into one of the children's empty bedrooms – putting her own dreams on hold and possibly her marriage at risk?

An interruption to any normal routine is fertile ground for a story. Just stop reading for a moment and think of a few. Think of some things in your life or the lives of the people around you that are taken for granted, and visualise what might happen if something happened to interrupt them.

Do it now!

I'll be surprised if you can't think of several interesting beginnings to stories without too much effort. Make a list of them somewhere in your notepad. There's no need to pursue any of them just yet, but you can never be sure when something like this will ignite a spark at a later date.

Now we'll move on to the next method of generating ideas.

A statement you'd like to make

All of us have things we feel passionate about, even if we normally don't have the time or the inclination to do much about it. You might, for instance, think that all politicians are corrupt, that the national health service needs improving, that richer countries exploit poorer countries, that morals are declining, that people are cruel to animals, that an overemphasis on political correctness is stifling initiative – or any one of a dozen other things. And thinking about any one of these concerns could start you off on a story.

All you have to do is personalise it. Create a character who's motivated in some way to take the kind of action you yourself might like to take if you only had the time, the courage and the opportunity. Or, conversely, create a character who displays some of the faults inherent in one of these problems and show that character getting their comeuppance. Sometimes we are so close to something that we don't realise its potential as a piece of drama.

I have personal experience of this. When I first broke into radio scriptwriting I was invited to talk to a producer about several ideas I had. (He had liked a sample script I sent him, but not enough to do it.) I enthusiastically 'pitched' about six ideas to him and he liked *none* of them. Just as I was about to leave his office he said he'd be delighted to hear from me again if I cared to come up with even *more* ideas.

I rather dejectedly said I didn't think I'd have the time. I told him I had a full-time job as a teacher and that my wife and I were fostering children as well as already having several of our own. Luckily I managed to refrain from saying that I had better things to do than think up stories that nobody was going to consider producing. He stopped me from leaving and said, 'Fostering? That might be an interesting subject for a comedy drama series.' We went on to do twelve half-hour episodes of my series *Growing Pains* on radio, and another twenty, fifty-minute episodes, on TV.

I hadn't even thought of mentioning fostering. It seemed so ordinary to me at the time but, when you think about it, what could be a better example of a routine being interrupted than welcoming other people's children into your home? I was just too close to see the possibilities at the time.

Interestingly, one of the best radio plays written by a student in one of my classes was about people shooting birds for sport. She had moved into a delightful country cottage and loved the rural simplicity and the peaceful surroundings. That was before she realised there was a regular 'shoot' in the area. She was shocked and appalled one day by the loud bangs from a dozen shotguns and by the sight of wounded birds falling to earth, sometimes almost into her garden. She imagined herself smuggling some of the healthy pheasants to safety and organising an escape route just like a wartime resistance fighter. She fantasised about saving so many of them that the shoot would become unprofitable and have to close down. And because she couldn't do it in reality she took some measure of satisfaction from doing it surreptitiously in fiction. At this moment the BBC still have the play under consideration. And I'll be as disappointed as she will be if they turn it down.

Maybe you have a pet hate, or an enthusiasm, that could be used in a successful way?

Think about it.

And so on to my third way of getting ideas.

Mood music

People who make TV commercials know how effective a piece of music can be. That's why so many adverts remain in our minds for decades, sometimes long after the product itself has ceased to exist. The same is true for certain films and television series. I only have to hear the opening bars of the Disney classic from *Pinocchio*, 'When you Wish upon a Star' and I am instantly transported back to the time I stood in a long queue outside the Gaumont Cinema in Derby over fifty years ago.

I'd like to bet that most people over the age of fifty-five can still recognise the introductory music for the TV series *Z Cars* (first shown in 1962). It had a rousing, almost military sound to it that made you instantly sit up and take notice.

Heartbeat used music from the 1960s and my own series, *Growing Pains*, used songs and music from the golden days of the Hollywood musical. *Heartbeat* was set in the appropriate era and for my own show I provided the reason (or excuse) that the main character was obsessed with musicals so that when we heard a song we were, in a way, hearing his unspoken thoughts. It was a lot of fun for me to choose suitable pieces, and a lot of fun for the excellent singers and musicians at the BBC to re-record them (it proved impossible to use the originals because of the high cost demanded by whoever held the rights to them in Hollywood). But it was also time consuming, and cost quite a lot of money.

All in all, it might be better for you either to ignore music altogether as far as your script goes or merely to suggest brief snatches of one particular piece or 'type' from time to time. I'm talking about background music here. If you are planning to write a calling-card script about a rock group or a boy or girl band you will know much more than I do on the subject and make your own decisions on it.

There is, however, one way in which I would strongly advise you to use music, and that's in giving yourself a kick-start with another writing exercise.

Sometimes I play music to my students to inspire them. I ask them to relax, close their eyes and imagine they are watching a film being shown on a large screen as they listen to whatever piece of music I play. After just three or four minutes I stop the music and ask them to write out their thoughts. The results are often surprising and gratifying.

Occasionally a seemingly cynical and tough young man who has previously written nothing for me but violent Quentin Tarantino-like scenes of murder and mayhem will come up with a tender and poignant love scene after listening to something like 'Smoke Gets in your Eyes' played by Larry Adler. Then I'll play something totally different, like parts of Tchaikovsky's *Nutcracker Suite.* Unlike the Larry Adler piece, which tends to produce quite similar results, the

Tchaikovsky music can produce widely differing ones.

Try it for yourself later. Select something from your own collection, perhaps two contrasting pieces, and listen to them in the way I've described. Listen to one piece and write about your thoughts, and then repeat the exercise with your second selection. Could you combine the two bits of writing into one idea? Or are they so different that you would need to develop them separately? It doesn't matter either way. It's just another exercise to get you thinking and writing.

It also doesn't matter that you might be listening to something you've already heard a thousand times before. You'll be listening to it in a new way. You may be surprised at how different and creative this kind of listening can be. And it *can* lead to an idea for a complete script.

So on to my fourth way of 'fishing' for ideas.

Borrowing from reality

Sometimes real life presents you with a plot that's already perfectly shaped as a story. You just have to recognise it and make a few changes to avoid embarrassing people. The more you think about it the more frequently it will happen. It's like having somebody paint your front door. Until that point you had barely noticed anyone else's front door, but all of a sudden you can't walk down a street without checking out the colour and condition of every door you see. Your attention is focused.

So get your attention focused on possible storylines for a thirty-minute TV piece. You'll find things cropping up all the time, sometimes trivial and funny and sometimes bleak and tragic. It's all part of life and you can't avoid it.

A student in one of my classes was having trouble getting started and said, despairingly, that he couldn't think of a single idea that hadn't already been done. I tried to reassure him that it isn't necessary to think of something totally original and that if he did it would probably involve a troupe of tap-dancing jellyfish or something equally bizarre. I talked about the fact that people are falling in love, climbing mountains, being made redundant, being killed in accidents, being mugged or having their hearts broken all the time, but this doesn't make these things boring when one of them happens to *you* or to someone you care about.

That's the secret. You have to *involve* the audience. Make your audience feel that the characters in your story are worth caring about. Then they stop being statistics and become people we know, if not ourselves.

If you can do this, anything dramatic that happens to your characters will be interesting and important and it won't matter how many times it's happened to other people in the past. Just think how many weddings take place in reality and how similar they are to each other, and then notice how viewing figures shoot up whenever there's a wedding in any of the popular soaps.

So don't waste time trying to think of something that's never happened. Just notice all the things that are actually happening all the time and just need a few twists and some personal involvement to make them work as drama or comedy.

Turning the Basic Idea Into an Outline

So far I've been talking about initial ideas, not story outlines. To turn your basic idea into an outline you need to look again at the basic story shape mentioned earlier. You need to know, as I've already said, that before embarking on an attempt at a script you have something with a beginning, a middle and an end. It isn't that difficult, and it can be fun juggling things around without the hard work of writing dialogue and creating situations in detail.

I've said that real life sometimes hands you a storyline in almost the perfect shape, so let me give an example of this. Someone I know (let's call her Louise) was studying at university and working very hard. So too were her friends, all except one (let's call her Sarah), who'd decided to party the nights away, skip as many lectures as possible and then buy her essays via the internet.

Naturally the hard-working Louise and her other friends got a bit fed up with this. It might have been a bit easier to bear if Sarah had kept quiet about what she was doing and given the others due credit for their honesty and effort, but she couldn't help teasing them about the situation. Being good friends, the other girls could hardly tell what they knew to their lecturers, or 'grass their friend up', as a soap character might describe it, but they did decide to teach her a lesson.

Louise took the initiative. She 'borrowed' some headed notepaper from the university office and an equally official-looking envelope. Then she wrote a letter to Sarah purporting to come from a senior lecturer, and posted it. In the letter she wrote that some serious doubts had been raised about Sarah's work practices and about the contents of some of her essays. She was required to come into the lecturer's office in a week's time to defend herself.

Louise and the others were suitably pleased by Sarah's dismay on reading the letter, and planned to let her stew for a few days before telling her the truth and before she actually spoke to anyone else about it. At first it worked beautifully; Sarah started attending lectures and making plans to write essays of her own in future. But then it went wrong. Sarah couldn't stand the strain any longer and went into the office earlier than she was supposed to do. The senior lecturer realised what must have happened and asked

Sarah if she had any idea who might play such a cruel trick on her. She knew precisely who'd done it but of course, for various reasons, didn't want to say so.

Meanwhile, Louise and the rest of her friends were wondering where Sarah was and getting a bit worried. Maybe they'd taken the joke too far and Sarah was even now climbing up to the top of the building to throw herself off?

That evening all was explained, with Sarah admitting that she had only got what she deserved and saying that she'd learned her lesson and would start acting with a bit more honesty and responsibility in future. (Especially since the senior lecturer – having been alerted unwittingly by herself – might now decide to keep a closer check on her just in case.) And there it might all have ended, but there was one more step to go. A few weeks later Sarah received another letter from the senior lecturer, and this time a genuine one, saying that in view of the trauma she'd suffered as the result of a stupid prank, her next set of assignments would be marked less rigorously than before. Sarah had come out on top once again.

It's not difficult to see how this whole fiasco could be turned into a one-page story outline, following the basic story shape, and then eventually into a complete script for an episode of a situation comedy. It practically writes itself, and scenes like the one where Sarah tries to explain her actions to the senior lecturer who doesn't know what she's talking about would be a gift for a comedy writer. It would be funny and satisfying.

On the other hand, it could all have been treated seriously with Sarah actually deciding she'd been caught out and taking an overdose. Or, yet again – getting back to the sitcom mood – perhaps Sarah, having talked to the lecturer without the other girls knowing, might leave a fake suicide note in their shared flat and let *them* suffer.

I'm sure you'll become aware of similar situations once you start focusing on real-life happenings through the eyes and ears of a writer.

Make a note

- Six ways to create ideas for story outlines (including the two you were invited to try as exercises in an earlier part of the book) are:
  – starting with a piece of random dialogue
  – inventing two characters and forcing them to interact
  – interrupting a routine
  – listening to music and visualising scenes
  – making a statement regarding a cause you are passionate about
  – borrowing from reality.

A First Go at an Opening Sequence

As already explained, the opening to any new TV show can be crucial. This means that the first few pages of your script need special care. If you don't interest the script-reader in the first few pages it's very unlikely that he or she will bother to read on.

Don't worry too much about it at this stage. Practising the writing of opening sequences can be great fun and totally worry-free. You know you can introduce something of great promise without having to follow through and write the whole thing. It's a bit like doing a pencil drawing of your dream house without ever having to build it. You can simply let your imagination take over so long as you keep things within reason and bear in mind all the restrictions mentioned earlier to do with locations, size of cast and costs in general.

Here's the first thing you ought to do. Make several copies of the opening three to five minutes of any show that seems appropriate: cop shows, hospital dramas, sitcoms or series dramas (like *Casualty*) but *not* ongoing soaps where the storylines will be following on from previous episodes. Pay particular attention to any brand new series, which will be trying to make an immediate impact and will be introducing totally new characters as quickly and effectively as possible.

See how much of the opening sequence is done visually and how much it's done with dialogue. Time each scene and see how many different scenes there are in the time slot you've decided on. Notice how one show differs from another. Think how you might have been able to improve some of them by rearranging the order of scenes or by shortening or lengthening them, by adding or subtracting dialogue or by adding or subtracting visuals.

Another good exercise is to stop a DVD you haven't watched before and try to guess what comes next. Then compare what you thought with what the writer did. The brilliant comedian and actor Brian Conley once told me he used to employ this stop/go technique when watching sitcoms or comedy sketch shows. He did this to improve his own understanding of how comedy works or doesn't work. Judging from the success he's had since then (he was given his own TV comedy series, *This Way Up*, when he was in his twenties and has won awards for both TV and stage performances) I'd say his hard-working approach is worthy of respect.

You should also notice that some shows have a stronger serial element than others. It's not always easy to say which show is part of a series and which is part of a *serial* since some shows that seem to be almost one-offs, like *Doctors*, also have a strong serial element too.

It isn't important at this stage that you can classify each show exactly: just be aware that there are subtle differences that will become important later, if and when you're invited to write a sample script for any of them.

So spend a few hours with your video player absorbing opening sequences. (Please note that the word 'sequence' just refers to an indefinite number of scenes following one after the other.) You might get ten scenes in the first five minutes or just one continuous scene, but for ease of understanding it could still be referred to as the opening sequence.

Here's a simple exercise for you to try. Look at the three sentences below. I've simply written down the first three fairly ordinary images that came to my mind. See if you can turn them into some sort of basis for an opening sequence. You've got to link them (or suggest links) and you can inter-cut from one to the other as often as you like and in whatever order you think suitable for whatever you have in mind. You might end up with three scenes or ten scenes. There's no need to make it look like a TV script. Just write it in prose as a series of descriptions that could later be turned into a properly shaped and detailed outline if required.

1. A man alone in a flat is looking at photographs.
2. An aeroplane taxis along a runway at a major airport.
3. A couple are shopping in a supermarket.

See what you can make of it. Just take five or ten minutes.

Do it now!

Here are the random connections that came immediately to *my* mind.

The man in the flat is a young white man. He's a university student. He is feeling sad as he looks at pictures of a young

Asian woman and himself taken at a student gathering.

We cut away to see the aeroplane move along the runway, having just landed.

From there we cut away to the supermarket, where an Asian couple are shopping and selecting items for a special meal. The man is happy and talking enthusiastically about making some expected guests welcome, but the woman is upset about something.

Back at the airport an Asian family are collecting their luggage from the carousel. There's a father, mother and their son who is in his early twenties.

Back at the flat the young white man is frantically trying to phone the Asian girl who turns out to be sitting on a bus – looking really miserable and ignoring her phone. The white boy is in love with the Asian girl and knows her parents are planning an arranged marriage for her.

That's as far as I got in ten minutes. I don't know if the Asian girl is heading home to her parents or running away, but I can see roughly where the story is going and I'm pretty confident I could turn this into an interesting opening sequence. Within six or seven quick scenes I could do all the things I've talked about with regard to the beginning of any story: introduce main characters, set location, tone and genre and provide a hook.

You can try this simple exercise any time you feel like it. Just write down three or four unconnected images and then see where your imagination takes you.

Of course, this is yet another simple way to generate story ideas – so perhaps you should add it to your previous list.

Make a note

- Record and study opening sequences.
- Decide for yourself what makes some work better than others.
- Make up your own opening sequences without thinking where they might lead.
- Use the stop/go technique to compare your own ideas with those of other people.
- Use the idea of three or four random settings to generate a new story idea.

A First Go at a More Complex Scene

So far we've been concentrating on scenes with just two people, or a sequence of scenes relying on a mixture of dialogue and visuals, but a writer is almost bound to meet situations in a script where several people are speaking together in a group. The potential problems here are basically three fold:

- Your scene is confusing and the main storyline gets lost.
- Several of your characters hold similar views so there's no variety.
- Some of your characters don't say anything and don't even react (because you, as the writer, didn't include them in the dialogue or action).

A good director will help you here by suggesting various reactions from non-speaking actors, and by pointing the camera in their direction at the appropriate time, but your script might never get that far if it doesn't look professional to begin with. You need to show you have a good overall grasp of things as well as being at the creative centre of it all.

Actually, it's not such a daunting prospect as it might at first appear. Often the introduction of third and fourth characters can give you a fresh slant on the proceedings and provide an extra surge of energy. You just need to make sure that they really *are* adding something fresh, and not just repeating what's already been said by one or another of the main characters.

I remember once being in a courtroom listening to a man giving a character reference for another man who'd been accused of theft. The character witness – let's call him Mr Smith – was introduced as a successful businessman, and certainly looked the part in his smart and expensive suit, his clean white shirt and silk tie. He answered the questions put to him by the defence solicitor convincingly and politely, and the members of the jury were impressed. He told how the accused man – a joiner – had done several jobs for him renovating properties and had always been honest and reliable. He said he'd be happy to give him more work should he be spared a jail sentence.

The duologue between the defence solicitor and the character witness was interesting enough but not exactly riveting, especially for the prosecuting solicitor who sat quietly wondering how he could counter this development. Things seemed to be going well for the accused. Then there was a dramatic intervention – just as you'd expect in a courtroom drama.

A junior solicitor who had been chatting quietly with a retired police officer in a corner of the courtroom suddenly approached the prosecuting solicitor and handed him a hastily scribbled note. A slow smile of relief spread across the prosecuting solicitor's face as he read the contents of the note. He stood up to make his response to the character witness. He was a good performer. 'Mr Smith, how kind of you to give up your valuable time to come here in support of a friend,' he said with a disarming smile. The character witness looked a bit less comfortable and said: 'I wouldn't exactly call him a *friend*.'

The prosecuting solicitor glanced at the note in his hand and then, looking thoughtfully first at the jury and then at the character witness, said, 'But Mr Smith, or can I call you, as most of your friends do, Liverpool George?' Then he paused to savour the man's sudden discomfiture before adding, 'Because isn't that what the defendant called you when you first met as fellow prisoners in Leicester Jail?' The spectators all burst into laughter as Mr Smith turned to his friend in the dock, shrugged his shoulders and said, 'Sorry, mate. I gave it my best shot.'

The introduction of a third and fourth party here certainly paid off in real life, just as it would in drama. So you'll see that, instead of fearing the task of dealing with a larger bunch of people, you can take a positive stance and see it as a golden opportunity to introduce a new angle and provide some new information.

Make a note

- Don't lose sight of the main storyline.
- Don't lose sight of characters on the page.
- Give each character something fresh to add to the proceedings.

Making sure that characters differ

Something that American sitcom writers talk about might be a useful thing to mention at this point. They sometimes look at their main characters and ask themselves if they've managed to make them differ enough – because characters who differ will create conflict, which is what you need in drama and comedy.

Someone came up with the idea of formalising this concept by deciding to have three distinct types they could classify as: a machine, an animal and a child. They didn't mean that literally, of course, this isn't science fiction or fantasy we're talking about, but ordinary people who can be categorised in these ways. The 'machine' might be a bright, intelligent person who is efficient and hardworking but a little bit cold and unemotional, a smart well-dressed person who starts things moving and can also finish them off or someone who generally plays things by the book. The animal, by contrast, would be a much more sensual person – someone who's impulsive and has a lively interest in sex, eating and drinking, and taking chances in life. And naturally the child would be innocent, unsophisticated and perhaps not too bright in understanding adult things.

You only have to take even a sideways glance at a series like *The Golden Girls* or *Cheers* to see how effective this kind of theory can be in practice, and to see how the three categories can be stretched or interwoven to create others. In *The Golden Girls* you have the slightly bossy and efficient Dorothy, the sexy Blanche and the dippy but lovable Rose, and there, surely, is an almost perfect example of the machine, animal and child theory in action. But take a closer look and you'll see Grandma, who's a bit of a mixture. She can be bossy like her daughter Dorothy but she is also more venal with a touch of Blanche and, because of her age, occasionally forgetful like Rose (but much more self-aware).

Similarly, in the equally excellent *Cheers* we have a machine of sorts in Frasier, an animal in Sam the ladies' man, and a child in Woody the simple barman. But again there are characters, like Cliff the anorakish mailman and Carla the shrewish waitress, who don't fit comfortably into either category and are perhaps a mixture of all three (as most people are in real life.)

Whether or not the original writers of these two series used the theory consciously, unconsciously, or not at all isn't really important. It is a helpful little 'trick' for a writer, and certainly one you might want to consider using and adapting. You might be able to come up with an even better set of character types yourself but, in the meantime, the important thing for you to remember is that you really do need to create contrasting characters for any drama or comedy.

Make a note

- Differing characters create conflict.
- Conflict is needed in drama and comedy.
- To ensure you have conflict you need contrasting characters.
- One way to create contrasting characters is to categorise them.
- Try the American idea of having a 'machine', an 'animal' and a 'child'.

Give each main character a biography

When I started writing my series *Growing Pains* for television I was advised to create a background for each of the main characters. This was to include date of birth, details about education, general interests and so on. Just a paragraph or two, nothing elaborate. A bit like the details you were asked to write before doing the second duologue exercise.

Robert McKee has a phrase he uses in his lectures about 'turning exposition into ammunition'. He explains that the more you know about a character's past experiences, the more you have to choose from when deciding on their present actions. 'Know your characters inside out' would be a shorthand way of putting it. My own view about this is that you can spend *too* much time on making up background material and stifle your own interest in the characters. It's nice to surprise yourself now and again or, more properly, allow the characters to surprise you.

You'll know your characters are really coming to life when they start refusing to do as they're told. This may sound a little crazy but there should be times when the plot requires one character or another to do something and you find you just can't write it. The character simply won't agree (in your mind) to do it, and if you go ahead anyway you find it doesn't work. This is not a moment to despair, it's a moment to rejoice, because it means you've created a character with a life of his or her own.

Anyway, let's put all this about creating contrasting characters together and use it in another little exercise. Take the American sitcom model of machine, animal and child and then add one made-up 'type' of your own – an unpleasant moaner, an irritating over-positive thinker, a prophet of doom, or whatever – and write very brief biographies for all of them.

Just to make it very clear, this means that you'll be creating *four* differing characters. Don't forget to give them suitable names, say where they come from, how old they are, something about their educational standards and their jobs and something about their favourite pursuits. Just take three or four minutes for each one – then come back to the book to see what to do next. Ready?

Do it now!

So now you have four characters in search of a story (or in this case a situation that could be part of a TV drama). Please remember that we're still just practising and having fun – nobody need ever see what you've written in these exercises unless you *want* to show them.

All we need to do now is place these characters in a location, let them talk and see what happens. Let's think of some situations that lend themselves to surprises and dramatic revelations. Choose one from the brief list below or make up one of your own:

- a reunion of some kind
- a séance
- a funeral
- a family gathering
- some kind of business deal
- quiz night in a pub or holiday hotel.

All you need to do, to give the story some sort of shape, is to choose a pivotal character, decide what they're hoping to get from this encounter and then give the story a twist so that things go wrong. Don't forget to let all the characters be themselves and play a full part in the proceedings, and don't try to tie it all up in too neat an ending. It's better to finish on a cliffhanger if you can – something that promises more action to follow.

Don't write for more than fifteen to twenty minutes and don't think too much about it *before* writing. Just try to write as if the words are coming out of your pen or pencil or through your keyboard and onto the computer screen, as if by magic.

Do it now!

Don't worry at all if you found that difficult and didn't come up with a sequence you were proud of. In a way that was the point of the exercise – to make you aware of how tricky it can be to handle larger groups of characters without losing some of them in the process. By the time you come to such a sequence in your first *real* attempt at a script you should know the characters well enough to know exactly what they'd say and *not* forget them.

How Character Biographies Can Push the Story Along

Another thing Keith Johnstone talks about in *Impro* is what he calls re-incorporation. He points out that sometimes it's wrong to look ahead to see where a story is going. It can be more fruitful to look *back* and check again with your character biographies. There you should find something that motivates one or another of your characters in such a way that it then becomes obvious what that character's next move would be.

Suppose, for example, you've written that a male character has been through a messy divorce? We might now reasonably expect that any woman he meets who gets close to him will be viewed with a certain amount of suspicion. And we'll *know* how he's likely to react if she casually mentions a dinner party she's been invited to – and told to bring a friend.

Similarly, Keith Johnstone says that the same reasoning applies to incidents that happen early on in your story. Sometimes you simply forget about them and leave loose ends, and at other times you don't even recognise their significance at first.

Make a note	• Things mentioned in your character biographies are like seeds waiting to flourish, so remember – if you're stuck for a way forward – don't be afraid to look back.

Raising the Stakes

Sometimes a storyline seems to get stuck in a rut and it's hard to see why. The main character is striving to achieve something and failing, but instead of being sympathetic and interested we become restless and bored. Often you'll find that this has happened because the problems the main character is facing have become stuck at the *same level.* He or she tries to overcome something and fails. Then they try again and fail again and we're back where we started.

What you need to do to overcome this problem is, as mentioned before, to *raise the stakes* and make the problems escalate as time runs out. Then the tension will increase and interest will not just be maintained but will rise accordingly. Also, when your pivotal characters fail they won't just go back to square one – they'll be stranded in some kind of no-man's land between success and failure, which means they just have to go on.

Suppose, for example, a happily married and ambitious couple have just found their dream home and calculate that they can just about afford to buy it *if* the husband can negotiate a slight increase on the annual rise he's expecting. The husband goes into the boss's office, only to be told the disastrous news that the company is struggling and, instead of a rise, he'll be asked to accept a reduction. That's a relatively small blow and something the husband might just shrug his shoulders about and be determined to overcome, but then suppose, on his way home, he's overtaken by a fire engine going to his house just too late to put out the blaze. The house is burnt to the ground and for some reason isn't covered by insurance. The husband is bravely trying to reassure his wife that they'll be able to cope, and that's when she tells him she's just found out that she's pregnant – with triplets.

I'm exaggerating to make a point, but I'm sure you can see what I mean. Even if you start with a real bang you can still raise the stakes higher when the pace of the story seems to slacken.

Make a note

- If the story seems to be stuck in a rut – raise the stakes.

The Difference Between Theme and Storyline

Let's keep this simple. If you hear people discussing a film or TV drama they've really enjoyed they will usually be talking about the story and what actually happened on screen.

It's quite rare to hear someone talk about the *theme* of anything, and when they do they'll probably hesitate and admit that they're not too sure – was it about triumph over adversity or about someone just getting back some of the luck they deserved? Was it really about a downtrodden woman finding the courage to leave her bullying husband or about a bullying husband who gets his comeuppance when his loving wife leaves him? Or was it entirely open to the viewer to make their own choice in the matter and still be 'right' about it?

So perhaps what we *really* mean when we talk about theme is depth – about the writer and performers trying to make the audience *think* about life rather than just be entertained for thirty minutes. It's not even possible to describe drama or comedy with depth as 'good', and shallow drama and comedy as 'bad', because who's to say that a successful *Carry-On* film isn't just as good (or better in many people's eyes) than a play by Shakespeare? It's like comparing fish and chips with *haute cuisine* and then having to admit that they both have their merits.

However, it is possible to recognise *certain* themes – like triumph over adversity – and also to realise that it's possible to keep the theme intact whilst changing the story completely. This same theme could apply to a drama about an athlete winning an Olympic gold medal or to a person of eighty finally learning to read and write. The story would be different but the theme would stay the same.

Perhaps it's enough for you to be able to recognise if your story has some sort of theme or not, even if you can't easily classify it. And maybe, in a sense, every story, like life itself, is at some level about triumph over adversity?

Just be aware that one day you might be in a script-editor's office and hear something like, 'I love the story but what would you say it's *really* about?' That's where it doesn't pay to say that you're not sure, or that it isn't about anything really – just a bunch of people doing interesting things. So even if you're not *sure*, try to say something that sounds profound (or at least shows that you gave it some thought!).

Make a note

- The story is *what* happens on the screen.
- The theme is to do with *why* it happens and the effects it might have at a deeper level (on characters and audience alike).

How to Analyse a Suitable TV Show

You've already been told how to analyse an opening sequence. Just extend this to a complete half-hour show, though you have to distinguish here between a BBC show and one shown on a commercial channel. Since we are aiming to write a thirty-minute piece without a commercial break I suggest you choose a suitable show from the BBC.

There can be a basic difference in shape between a show without commercials and one with them. For a start, a thirty-minute BBC show really does last for thirty minutes or almost that length of time, whereas a show for a commercial channel will be closer to twenty-four minutes. In addition, a show for a commercial channel is likely to have some kind of mini-cliffhanger just before the midway advertising break. This is, of course, to hook the audience into not switching over. Then the story has to be introduced all over again. Since we are concentrating on a show without commercials (to avoid unnecessary confusion for new writers) you can simply forget about this aspect of TV writing at the moment. The important thing is that you complete your calling-card script and make it as convincing as possible.

So, just to make it clear, choose a thirty-minute show you like – either sitcom, soap or drama – and record it. Play it scene-by-scene and write down (in prose) in your notepad a brief account of what happens. There's no need to write down the actual dialogue if you don't want to but it can be a useful exercise to do this for at least *some* of the scenes. It can certainly be useful to count the lines of dialogue in each scene (and by that I don't mean sentences, I mean speeches). So if a character says a single word it counts as one line and, similarly, if he or she says several sentences, without being interrupted, this still counts as one 'line'. It's the number of 'exchanges' that is important here.

This will also show you clearly how different characters use different speech patterns. It can make you very aware of how speech in real life, and in dramas that are based on real life, doesn't flow 'correctly' as it might in the pages of a classic novel (and almost certainly in your early attempts at scriptwriting).

Notice also how the story threads are spaced out and how the scenes vary (if they do). Is a duologue followed by a larger cast scene, and is a quiet scene followed by a noisy one? Is an interior scene followed by an exterior one and vice-versa? Are some scenes longer than others? One of the things that makes a script seem dull is when the scenes are all of equal length and tone, one long talky scene, followed by another long talky scene and so on. Even when such scenes are well written *individually* the piece as a whole can appear monotonous. To keep your viewers on their toes you need to break up the rhythm.

Make a note

- To avoid monotony, scenes in a TV drama, sitcom or soap need to be varied.
- They can be made:
  – longer or shorter
  – more talky or less talky
  – with a small cast or larger cast
  – indoors or outdoors
  – angry and loud or quietly reflective
  and so on ...

Don't just do this analysis once, record a totally different show and see how much it differs from the first. And once you get into this kind of analysis you might want to stop the tape at various points, as you were advised to do with the opening sequence analysis earlier, and see if you can predict what scene or scenes will follow.

The more you're prepared to do this kind of thing the more you'll learn. The point of this is not so that you can slavishly copy other people's methods, but that one day soon you'll know enough about the basics to create a style of your own. This is exactly the kind of thing great artists, athletes and musicians have always done, but also remember that a wise person once said, 'Over analysis leads to paralysis', and never stop trying to create your *own* characters and ideas.

You might be interested to know that scenes in TV shows seem to be getting shorter all the time. When I started writing for TV some twenty-five years ago most thirty-minute pieces might have just four or five long scenes. My friend John Temple, who was once producer of *Coronation Street*, tells me that he would routinely expect each episode to have five or six scenes before the commercial break and a similar number afterwards, giving an average total of twelve scenes per episode. Now you'll regularly see shows with thirty to forty scenes in that time.

Please note: there are always exceptions to every rule and a few shows, like the success *The Royle Family*, are prepared to go against the trend and have long scenes in a fairly static situation. But it's fair to say that these exceptions are rare. Maybe the fashion will swing back again – just keep watching and analysing.

Counting the Cost: Characters, Location, Setting

There is a misconception amongst many students of writing that certain aspects of recording a TV show are simple to do and cost nothing. A parent parking a car in a supermarket car park, getting out with a couple of children and walking towards the place where the trolleys are kept, for example. Something we see in real life all the time, and which we could probably film ourselves on video without too much trouble and certainly without incurring any payment.

However, this is not usually how it works for a TV crew making a professional drama, who need to control what's happening in and around the immediate area. They might want to stop the flow of traffic to set up cameras and sound recording equipment and maybe fix up some extra lighting. They'll also want to avoid spectators waving at the cameras or trying to obtain autographs from the actors. They'll even be hoping that an aeroplane won't fly overhead at an inappropriate moment, and so on.

All this is to get the quality of sound and vision they need for transmission. And sometimes the simplest scene like this can take hours – hours of intruding on someone else's business – and that will often have to be paid for in hard cash. And this can go on for day after day. Sometimes a whole day can be taken up just to shoot two or three minutes of broadcastable material.

The cost can really escalate if the location is a long way from the actual studio. The cast and crew might have to be taken there and then fed and watered at lunchtime, which will involve the use of a mobile catering firm. And if your script calls for night-time filming it gets even more complicated. It's more difficult to film in a fading light, so that will take extra time and the crew will be on overtime. If filming goes on very late into the evening then cast members might have to stay in a hotel nearby rather than returning home – and again this costs money.

Similarly, indoor scenes either need to be shot in real buildings – which someone usually owns and will require payment for – or will have to be constructed in the studio as sets. The more elaborate these sets are, the more costly it will be.

Making TV programmes is a very expensive business and you need to show in your script that you're aware of this. As a general rule, don't expect *anything* to be done easily or cheaply.

6

Some Tricks of the Trade

One-minute Overview

In this chapter the focus will be on some of the technical elements involved in scriptwriting. You'll find out what a TV script looks like and why. Various aspects of script layout will be explained in detail. You'll learn about 'scenes within scenes'. You'll be told about the importance of not setting your drama in some kind of TV never-never-land. You'll be shown the how, when and where of describing characters in your script. You'll learn what is meant by 'turning exposition into ammunition'. You'll be given some ideas on finding suitable names for characters. You'll be told how to handle scene transitions smoothly and how to begin and end scenes in the most effective way possible. You'll be shown how a cheap and simple 'establishing shot' can save hours of effort and expense. But you'll also learn how a deceptively 'easy' thing, like an on-screen telephone call, can present problems to a writer. And once again something will be said about the dynamics of a scene (this time a more complex scene) and how it fits into the piece as a whole.

What a Script Looks Like and Why

Roughly speaking, a scene is a continuous piece of recording that takes place in one setting. The scene doesn't end when the actors we're following at that particular time leave it to go elsewhere and another group of actors come in to take their place – or when the focus switches from one group to another – but when the cameras stop filming and *have to be moved* to another set. However, this could alternatively happen when other cameras, already set up in another location, come into action.

Scene endings and beginnings are easy enough to spot on screen, when the action switches from an interior studio set to an exterior location and back again, but it isn't always this clear cut. As mentioned earlier, some studio sets will be built in such a way that a character can move from, say, the lounge area of a house to the kitchen, and still be in range of the cameras via an open doorway or a serving hatch. This won't require a scene change.

Many sets are, however, single rooms laid out next to other sets like large cubicles, each with only three walls (as explained earlier), and these sets won't necessarily be in any realistic kind of order. Someone's lounge might be right next to an office that's supposed to be in another town. And right next to that might be a flat that's supposed to be at the top of a skyscraper. All of them will be at floor level inside a large studio space – like part of a warehouse.

Have you ever wondered why you nearly always see the main room of the Rover's Return in *Coronation Street* from the same or similar angles? Why you rarely if ever see the wall that would be to the left of the bar as you enter the room from the street? It's because most sets only have three complete walls and have to be viewed from a certain angle.

So, in general, a scene starts in a certain place and finishes when the cameras have to move to another place entirely – not merely to another spot on the same set. You have to be aware that the camera can move from group to group within the same set and it will still count as the same scene. You see this a lot in the Rover's Return and The Queen Vic in *Eastenders.* The camera may start by showing us a single person at the bar talking to a barmaid and later swivel to pick up on a group of others sitting at the table near the door, but this will be classified as one scene. The scene only ends when the action moves from that bar to a completely different set altogether.

On occasions when two or more completely separate story threads are being followed in the same room, and it's written in the script as one scene, this is for *technical* reasons rather than artistic ones. Common sense would seem to suggest that *artistically* a scene ends when one group of people finish their discussion, and we pick up on a different group involved in another discussion, but in fact scripts are broken up into separate scenes for the benefit of the technical crew, rather than the actors.

That's why script-editors, producers and directors like you to start each new scene on a new page. There's a good reason for this. Scenes are rarely, if ever, shot in chronological order. Suppose you have written a script with thirty scenes and used just two indoor sets and several different outside locations? It makes good sense to separate all the scenes into groups according to sets and locations and film them accordingly. So the crew may spend several days filming all the scenes that take place in one set before moving on to do the same with another set. This avoids the bother of flitting from one set to another trying to film things in sequence. (This would probably be better for the actors, who could follow the emotional flow of the script much more easily doing it this way, but not for anyone else.)

The real difficulty for a new writer is in trying to guess whether some of the sets will be multiple or not, or if a real building will be used where it *might* be possible to follow a character from one room to another. I think it's easier to assume that every room and every corridor is a single set and write with that in mind.

When the character we're following opens a door and moves out of shot you write **CUT TO**: and then type in a page break (using **Enter** and **Ctrl** together). Then you start the next scene on a new page.

If the director sees a way to shoot it as a single scene he or she will have no problem in just ignoring your new scene heading and carrying on, but they will be irritated if you take the other approach and they find themselves reading something they can't film and have to start tearing pages in half or asking for material to be rewritten. It's not likely to get that far, but it's still irritating for a director if he or she has to ask for simple rewrites that can disrupt the page numbers of the script and might cause confusion.

Scenes Within Scenes

Sometimes it's a good idea to use the term CUT TO: when you want the focus of interest to move from one group of characters to another within the same room – as described above in public places like bar rooms. Instead of writing something like, 'We now focus on another group in the same room' you simply finish whatever you want to say with regard to one group and then drop down a space or two and write 'CUT TO': You then describe who or what we are seeing now – but *without* the need to write a new scene heading. To avoid any possible confusion I suggest you don't underline the 'internal' CUT TO:s and don't type them in bold.

I also suggest you use them very sparingly or it will look as if you are trying to do the director's job by saying where you want the cameras to be pointed. It's best to use this internal CUT TO: only when one group in the same room or location isn't directly connected to the first group, in which case it really is a new 'scene within a scene'.

If, however, you've introduced a small group of people in a bar, for example, and got them talking, and then the door opens and two more people come into the bar intending to join that group, there's no need to do a CUT TO: here. The original scene is continuing. You merely write, in the directions, that the door has opened and that two more people have come into the room (and include their names if appropriate) and the director will angle the camera shots accordingly.

Outdoor Scenes

In trying to decide what exactly indicates a change of scene and what doesn't it can be even more confusing when dealing with *outdoor* scenes and sequences.

Suppose we are watching a school football match? Various cameras may be set up around the pitch to capture shots on goal at either end, and another camera to record the conversations and reactions of spectators, much as they would be at a 'real' match. But will it be written and shot as one continuous scene or not? Here again, we can see that dramatically and artistically even a few minutes could be split up into separate scenes: the scoring of the goal, the cheers or arguing amongst the spectators, a time-jump perhaps to the other team scoring the equaliser, and so on.

All this *could* and probably would be treated as one continuous scene, because any changes of camera angle and so on could be done swiftly and without much of a break.

Obviously, if the picture on screen moved from the pitch to the inside of a changing room and back again it would require scene changes, but as long as the action takes place in the same general area – within range of the camera – then it won't. A certain amount of common sense (and maybe even guess-work) is needed here because although a football pitch on a playing field covers a large area it is still self contained and a recognisable 'unit', whereas a farm or a hikers' trail might not be.

That's where you have to make a decision. Try to visualise yourself as the director in these situations. Can you imagine setting up the cameras in a particular way and not having to move them? Would you be able to oversee all that's going on from your own vantage point or would that be impossible? Would you need to stop working in one place and move to another?

Don't be too scared by all this. Even experienced writers find it difficult, and they will often have to rewrite sections of the script to cope with it – or they'll find the director has made his or her own decisions in the matter. You simply have to do your best and make the script look as professional as possible.

Changes are going to be made anyway. Something you wrote as having twenty scenes can quite easily end up having thirty without a word of your dialogue being altered. Characters will just move around more, and if it works really well you'll benefit, because nobody in the audience will know that's not exactly the way you wrote it.

- TV scripts are written in scenes for practical purposes rather than artistic ones.
- A scene ends when the action moves and the cameras can't simply follow.
- This applies to both indoor and outdoor sequences.
- The phrase **CUT TO:** is used mainly to signal the end of a scene, but you can use CUT TO: to signal a change of focus within a scene.

The Actual Layout of a Script

The first thing you'll notice about a script written for television is that the wide left-hand margin, usually almost half the page, is left blank. That wide margin space is used by the director. It's where he'll write (in pen or pencil) his notes on camera angles to correspond to the actions and dialogue of the characters. Later on the script will be re-typed by a secretary, as mentioned earlier, to include these notes in a more formal way.

All this seems to make perfect sense, but in fact the wide margin isn't really necessary at the very first stage because if your script is accepted it will invariably be re-typed to conform to that particular company's (or show's) style. It seems that almost every show has minor variations in the way its scripts are formatted – to do with the positioning of character names, the size and style of font, the line spacing and so on. So in theory writers might be allowed to save on postage and paper by simply writing their initial scripts in a simpler style – using the full width of the page and without the need to start each scene on a new page.

For some reason, however, this is discouraged. Maybe a lot of TV executives hold shares in the Post Office. But whatever the reason, your initial script is supposed to look as much like the 'real' thing as possible. In fact, the really important thing is that your script is easy to read and consistent, so that there is no confusion over dialogue and directions or where the action is taking place.

The example given in the appendix is of just one particular 'house' style, and there are exact instructions for you to use in setting up shortcut keys to help you achieve it as simply as possible. This is as good a layout as any for you to use. Don't worry if the instructions seem a bit complicated at first – they are relatively simple to follow and once in place will make the typing of your script flow much more easily. Try it later and see.

Scene Headings

It is important that you start each scene correctly, so here's an example of a very short scene (not with correct margin settings at this point) with some explanations.

SCENE 4. EXT. PAULA'S HOUSE. DAY. 08.21

[PAULA IS STANDING ON THE DRIVE NEAR HER CAR WITH REAR DOOR OPEN. HER CHILDREN, ROSS AND LORRAINE, COME INTO VIEW READY FOR SCHOOL.]

PAULA:
(IRRITATED) Quickly please.

[THE CHILDREN LOOK AT EACH OTHER AS THEY START TO GET IN WITHOUT HURRYING.]

CUT TO:

The scene heading is very important. Every time you start a new scene you write a heading like this with at least four bits of information *coming in the same order*:

a) The scene number.
b) Whether it's interior or exterior (INT or EXT).
c) The exact location, and this should remain consistent – so **PAULA'S HOUSE** must always be *precisely* that. You mustn't call it something else in another scene. If she lives with a partner called Bill you don't call it BILL'S HOUSE. This would cause confusion as people would think it was a new location.
d) Whether it's DAY or NIGHT.

The fifth bit of information:

e) The exact time. This can be considered optional. Some shows find it useful but others don't think it's necessary. They are happy to work within the approximations of DAY or NIGHT, or perhaps variations such as EARLY MORNING or LATE

EVENING and so on. I'd suggest you have nothing to lose by using the exact timing in your calling-card script, and it is a useful way of focusing your mind on the realities of what can and can't happen within a given time period.

Directions

These used to be called 'stage directions' because drama scripts were originally written for the stage, and as far as I know nobody has yet come up with a more suitable name for these instructions for actors and crew. The word 'directions' on its own can be a bit confusing, but that's the way it is.

Beneath the scene heading there should *always* be a brief 'set-up' (directions) telling us who is there and what they are doing – even if it's just a hallway with one person talking into a phone. You can't just start with dialogue and expect the actors to work things out for themselves.

As always, the important thing to remember is that a script should be easy to read and understand. You need to make sure there's no confusion between actions and dialogue or who's saying what. It's common sense really.

Speakers' Names

Another very important thing is to do with character names when used to denote who is speaking. If you start by calling a person Paula you must always use that name as a heading. Other people may refer to her as Mrs Smith or Prime Minister or Mummy, but she will always appear before her lines of dialogue as **PAULA:** and the same rule applies for all the other characters.

You may notice that I *didn't* choose to start with **SCENE 1** in the above example. The reason for this is because I would then have had to give a brief description of each character. Since I'll be dealing with this later I want you to assume these characters have already been introduced in an earlier scene. Here I just want to concentrate on the layout.

Make a note

- A script is split up into scenes just as a book is divided into chapters.
- Each new scene begins on a new page.
- There will always be a brief 'set-up' after the scene heading.
- The scene heading will always contain at least four bits of information (as shown).
- They should always appear in the same order.
- These four items are enough for your calling-card script, though you can include the exact time if you want to
- Once a name has been chosen for a location it must stay the same.
- Names used to indicate who is speaking don't change either.
- Leave a wide margin on the left and don't cram too many lines on each page.
- Try not to split up dialogue speeches over a page.
- Refer to script layout instructions (in the appendix).

The Importance of Exact Location

Many aspiring scriptwriters seem to take the view that dramas and comedies aimed at British TV can be set in some kind of strange TV never-never-land that doesn't have to be specified. It can be disconcerting to find several of the characters talking about sidewalks, gas stations and hit men – and suddenly realise it's supposed to be set in Chicago and not an English town as you would, quite reasonably, imagine.

Maybe this reluctance to specify an exact location is some kind of throwback to the days when most actors and most studios were based in London, so it was easier to find locations there and to find actors who sounded right – with a slight London accent or with barely any accent at all. Indeed, in the very early days of British film and TV, many actors had elocution lessons, presumably to make their speech easier to listen to and understand. Character actors like Thora Hird and Dora Bryan stuck out like a sore thumb and deservedly became icons.

It could be quite amusing to hear well-trained actresses from London with perfect BBC accents trying to play factory girls from Lancashire opposite more natural performers like George Formby. 'Oh Mummy,' they'd say, 'George is taking me out *dahncing* this evening and I simply don't have a thing to wear. Isn't it simply too frightful for words?' To which someone like Formby or Thora Hird would reply, 'There's nowt wrong wi' them clogs, lass, so stop mithering. Just you geroff out and enjoy thisen.'

We've come a long way since those days, and the London bias isn't nearly so pronounced. You'll see shows set all over the British Isles, though perhaps still principally in certain areas: Manchester, Liverpool, Newcastle, Birmingham and so on, with few glimpses of other places like Leicester and Derby (though the Peak District figures quite often) and large parts of Wales.

When I first wrote *Growing Pains* for radio it was supposed to be set in Derby where I live, but I was quickly told this wasn't really practical. The main recording studios were in London and it would be difficult to get enough actors with convincing Derby accents. As I'd already suggested Ray Brooks as the male lead and Sharon Duce as his wife, after seeing them work so well together in a TV series called *Big Deal*, and as they were both based in London, the decision was obvious. The series was set in London, though interestingly Sharon Duce actually comes from Yorkshire.

But the point is that I'd given a lot of thought to where the show was set. I hadn't just assumed that one town in England is pretty much like any other, and you must take the same attitude. Know where it's set and make that clear from the start. Be aware that people in a small town in North Yorkshire are unlikely to have exactly the same behaviour and speech patterns as people in a large city like London.

Let me reiterate something I mentioned much earlier. Your calling-card script should almost certainly be set in a familiar location – somewhere you know well and your viewers will recognise. To give it authenticity you, as writer, ought to have a very clear idea exactly what town, village or at least county you are thinking about. It doesn't matter at all that your chosen location may undergo a name change to avoid possible confusions over 'real' happenings and 'real' people in a particular place. You have to know where it is you're writing about, and so do the actors and crew, even if it's never actually stated to the audience.

We all know that 'Walford' doesn't really exist but we accept it as being part of London's East End, (and the name of the series *Eastenders* gives us quite a clue!) Similarly we accept that 'Weatherfield' in *Coronation Street* is supposed to be part of Manchester and, although it's sometimes criticised for being rather 'stagey' and old fashioned, it still convinces because it remains consistent. This would not have happened if the original writer hadn't had a really firm idea of where the place was supposed to be and peopled it accordingly.

Make a note

- Your location ought to be fairly exact, even if it has a false name.
- You can give it a fictitious name if necessary but you must know where it is.
- The producer and others will also need to know this.
- Convincing drama or comedy drama doesn't take place in a vacuum.

Where, When and How Do You Describe Characters?

The names of your main characters should appear near the beginning of your script in a character list. This should give the briefest of details: name and age only – or name, age and relationship to the main character if necessary (see script example in appendix).

You may add at the bottom something like 'Various non-speaking extras', but only the main speaking characters are really important at this stage and, incidentally, if you have more than about eight of them in a thirty-minute script a script-editor or producer may be put off straight away and not bother to read any further.

Keep the beginning of your script simple and uncluttered. Your objective is to get someone reading the creative stuff, not giving up on the technicalities. For that reason I rarely bother to give a breakdown of locations at the beginning of my own scripts. As I say, I want the reader to start turning the pages and getting hooked by the dialogue, the characters and the story. If you can get them involved in this way then maybe they'll suggest changes to cast and locations later – but if they don't even read the script you've got no chance whatsoever.

I sometimes have a 'blurb' on the second page of the script. (Again you can see an example of this in the appendix of this book). This doesn't give many details of the story – and certainly not the ending. It's a little 'teaser' designed to draw a reader in. 200 - 250 words is plenty.

So if you don't write descriptions of characters at the beginning of the script, where *do* you write them? You write them individually, in the actual body of the script, at their first point of entry – see Chapter One. To remind you: 'Mike is middle aged. A tough-looking man with the personality of a Rottweiler.' That's enough. You may have three or four others to introduce on the same page. It can be a bit tedious but it's essential. One day, if you're successful, an actor will have to be cast for each part and he or she will need something to base their performance on.

Just keep it brief and then get on with the action or the dialogue. You may have to describe the character again later if his or her appearance has changed in some way or if they are wearing something we wouldn't expect – but generally the first time is enough.

Make a note

- List your main characters at beginning of script.
- Describe them briefly at first point of entry.

Character Biographies: Turning Exposition Into Ammunition

If you only describe your characters very briefly in the script, what do you do with the character biographies we discussed earlier?

Firstly, you use them for your own information – so you can get to know your characters inside out – and then you use them to make the story more layered with meaningful detail. Remember the phrase used by Robert McKee about turning exposition into ammunition? The more you understand about your characters the more you'll be able to see them as fully-rounded people and not stereotypes. If you are using their past mistakes, interests and successes to enliven their present thoughts and actions it will be apparent in the way the characters behave. You won't need to spell it out separately.

Don't send the character biographies out with your calling-card script. It's very unlikely that they'll be given much attention, if any at all. Most people who want to be writers can produce reams of stuff about characters at the drop of a hat. It's putting it to good use in a script that's the difficult part. But don't throw these character biographies away. There's just a chance that a script-editor or producer will ask questions about your characters or even ask to see your background material. So keep it safely on your computer or disk (or both) and perhaps keep printed-off copies too.

Make a note

- Keep character biographies and other background material somewhere safe, but don't send this material out unless someone specifically asks to see it.

Finding Suitable Names for Characters

If you're one of those people who can think up names that immediately bring a character to life you can count yourself fortunate. Most writers struggle with names. I'm one of them. I can spend days trying to think of a name that makes a man sound important and end up calling him Mr Strong.

Luckily it's not the most important thing in a script, but it must be a delight to invent a name like Ebenezer Scrooge that fits the part so perfectly that part of it enters the language as a descriptive noun. Sometimes I think Dickens went well over the top with the names he invented: the Cheeryble brothers, Captain Cuttle, Mr M'Choakumchild and so on. He used words that seemed to suggest a character trait, or an object associated with the person's job or personality, and then twisted them slightly.

This is a trick worth considering and Uriah Heep, Volumnia Dedlock, Mr Fezziwig, Bradley Headstone and, incredibly, over 900 other names Dickens invented for his characters are well worth looking at. All you need to do is type the words 'Dickens character names' into your internet search engine and wait to be inspired.

Note the forename Bradley, which is more often used as a surname. This is another way to give a slightly unusual emphasis to a character's name. We've probably all heard of people with Warren, Bradley or Chandler as forenames but what about Walker, Bentley or Cooper? Just take a look at the names in your local telephone directory and see if they could be switched around.

Roy Clarke is a modern writer who is worth studying in this respect. What better name for a snobbish woman could you come up with than Mrs Bucket (which she insists on pronouncing Bouquet)? And to make it even funnier Roy gives her the first name Hyacinth. Hyacinth Bouquet! Just perfect. In the same show in which Hyacinth Bucket appears, *Keeping Up Appearances*, the scruffy and terminally lazy brother-in-law is called Onslow. It makes him sound unique and he is. I presume that's a name Roy Clarke invented purely for this character and I believe it's a village somewhere in Yorkshire.

So Roy seems to have come up with another useful way of naming characters – by using place names from the appropriate locality but as Christian names rather than surnames.

In another of his shows, the phenomenally successful *Last of the Summer Wine*, the late and very popular actor Bill Owen was perfectly cast as 'Compo', a man who always looked as if he'd just come from a hard day's work on a building site (compo being a term used by builders to describe the mixture of sand and cement more properly called mortar). - Then there was Marina, a giggly and flirtatious middle-aged woman who dresses and behaves like a flirty teenager, and her romantic but married suitor Howard. Two more names that seem entirely appropriate.

Thinking along these lines, I came up with the idea of *combining* a couple of these ideas to produce a variation of my own. I thought of using the place name in the locality as a forename, and using an object to do with a job as a surname. Quite clever, I thought. Unfortunately, all I've managed to think of so far is 'Lester Keyborde' for a man who's an East Midlands journalist and 'Sandiacre Bedpan' for the girlfriend he first met on a visit to the local hospital. As I said, it isn't one of my strengths. Maybe it'll work better for you?

It isn't easy thinking up names that make an impact but, as Dickens showed long ago and Roy Clarke is still showing, it is possible.

Make a note

- Try to create interesting names by:
  - twisting a word that suggests a characteristic
  - turning common surnames into unusual Christian names
  - using place names from the relevant geographical area
  - trying a combination of these things.

Come to think of it, isn't that how names were created in the first place – through characteristics, place names and occupations?

Handling Scene Transitions Smoothly

Now that you understand more about what constitutes a scene, and what doesn't, we need to consider how best to move from one scene to another.

Technically, as you've already been told, this isn't at all difficult for the writer. You merely write **CUT TO:** at the point where you want that scene to end, move on to a new page and write your new scene heading. Artistically, however, deciding *exactly* at which point it's best to leave one scene and start another is a different matter. Even scenes that appear to have a very obvious stopping point aren't quite that simple.

Ending scenes effectively

Suppose a man and woman are arguing and the woman goes out of the room in a fury, after hurling some final insult at the man, slamming the door behind her – obviously a good point at which to end that scene and move on to another one. But don't be too hasty to write **CUT TO:** after the direction SHE SLAMS THE DOOR SHUT. Effective as a slamming door might be, it's still not as telling as the impression it's made on the person still in the room. Is he smiling ruefully, blazing with anger or close to tears? And *that's* what we really want to see. That's what will give us a clue to what's going to happen later. A slammed door suggests finality, but what does a door know?

So always think carefully about the effect you're hoping to have on the audience and end the scene accordingly. You can simply write: DAVE LOOKS DEVASTATED or, conversely, DAVE STANDS EXRESSIONLESS FOR A MOMENT AND THEN GIVES A SHOUT OF TRIUMPH. HE'S GOT WHAT HE WANTED. You can see what a difference this can make. Don't end the scene prematurely. Get the most out of it.

Scene beginnings

The opposite is often true of scene beginnings. New writers tend to put too *much* into them and write the scene as if the new surroundings need to be properly introduced to the audience. Suppose, for example, we are moving to a scene where two people are meeting in a bar. We don't need to see them come into the bar, order drinks, stand waiting as the barman fills two glasses, hand over cash and wait for the change. Yes, this is what happens in reality but the viewers already know that. They want you to get on with the story.

So when you're wondering how to begin such a scene *don't* think to yourself, 'Ah, what happens when we go into a bar? Oh I know. We go to the bar and order drinks...' because this *isn't* reality. Drama, as somebody once said, is reality with all the boring bits left out.

Think instead: 'Now what do I need to do to keep the plot moving? Oh I know. I need one character to tell the other he's having problems raising the money he'd promised to pay up ...' or whatever. Then you jump straight into it with both people already seated at a table in the corner with drinks already in front of them. One character is feeling scared and the other about to get vicious – we can feel the tension in the atmosphere straight away. We don't need to hear a barman say, 'That'll be four pounds twenty, lads' to add authenticity.

Focus more on the needs of the story – and less on making the background authentic. The audience care more about the main characters and the emotions than the reality or otherwise of the setting.

Beginning a scene with a different character

Another thing that can make scene transitions appear awkward is when you end and begin consecutive scenes on the same character. This can work well sometimes – to show the passage of time in an 'arty' way perhaps – but in ordinary circumstances it can give a jerky and slightly unnatural look to the proceedings, as if your character is jumping from one place to another like someone taking part in a conjuring trick.

You achieve a better and more natural flow by cutting away from your main character and opening up with a different character. It can be the person your main character is going to meet or simply a non-speaking extra: a doorman at a hotel, a secretary sitting in an office, or whatever. And *then* we see the main character either already in the place or just arriving. That way they won't appear to have arrived by magic in the blink of an eye.

Make a note

- Don't *end* scenes a few seconds too early.
- Don't *begin* scenes a few seconds too early.
- Think in terms of story first and reality second.
- Try not to begin and end consecutive scenes on the same character.

The establishing shot

Another thing that can prove awkward is cutting away from a room in a particular house – the kitchen, for instance – to a bedroom that looks as if it could easily be in the same house but is in fact supposed to be somewhere on the other side of the world. A good way to do this is by using something called 'an establishing shot'. Instead of going directly from one interior to another you insert between these two interior shots an *exterior* shot of the second building, to set the new location (hence the word 'establishing') before moving inside. This makes it clear that we haven't just moved from one room to another inside the same building, but that we have moved location – perhaps even to another town.

In reality it's very unlikely that the establishing shot will have anything to do with the interior shot that follows. If you've ever seen *The Golden Girls* you'll know that they're supposed to live in Florida, and that is indeed the place where the house used for the establishing shots actually is. But the show itself is filmed thousands of miles away in California inside a studio. It's possible that some of the regular performers have never even been to Florida. It doesn't matter – the illusion that they are all living inside a house in Florida works very well. That's what a good establishing shot can do.

It can work equally well in a smaller way – showing that a house is in the Lake District perhaps, rather than a suburb of London. And if there's no dialogue or action involving your characters it doesn't have to be too difficult or expensive. The very same 'still' shot can be used time and again (for several years in the case of a long-running series). Just think of that shot of the rooftops at the back of a row of terraced houses that introduces each episode of *Coronation Street*. Establishing shots can be used in your opening sequence to great effect, showing us where your main characters live, work or play. They don't have to be reserved for bridging the gaps between one interior scene and another.

Even if nothing happens in your establishing shot, and it's just a static photograph, it will still be written as a separate scene and numbered accordingly every time it's shown.

Telephone calls

The first time I included a phone call in one of my scripts I thought it would be very simple to write. The two-way conversation began like this: 'Hello', 'It's me', 'You're late', 'I know – sorry I've been really busy' – and already I'd used four separate scenes by dodging backwards and forwards between the pair of them. By the time their fairly brief conversation ended I was on the eleventh scene of a sequence lasting about a minute. Not only was it tedious to write but it was a terrible waste of paper! I vowed never to do that again, and I now teach my students how best to avoid it too.

Basically there are four different ways of handling a phone call in a TV drama:

1. We see *and* hear just one of the characters and fill in the blanks ourselves.
2. We stay with one character and *hear* the voice of the other via the phone.
3. We see and hear both characters – flitting between one location and the other.
4. We see and hear both characters at the same time using a split-screen image.

The first of these options is, technically speaking, the simplest to write. You are just describing what one person is doing and saying. This works very well when the conversation is very brief.

The second option is still fairly simple. You describe what one person is doing and saying but you also include dialogue for the person we can't see. You write the dialogue for both characters as normal but add something to the unseen person's dialogue to make it clear that he or she isn't appearing on the screen, simply writing something like: **JOHN:** (OOV) Hello ... (and so on). OOV is short for 'out of vision'.

The third and fourth options can be written in a similar way to each other. You start with one character making a call in a setting that's already had a scene heading and been described and then **CUT TO:** another scene where – after the scene heading and directions – you describe the character receiving the call. You have now established *both* settings for the conversation that follows, and instead of bouncing from one scene heading to another (as I did in the early days) it is now acceptable to simply write something like: (WE NOW MOVE FROM ONE CHARACTER TO ANOTHER AS AND WHEN APPROPRIATE.) Similarly, for the fourth option you would write: (WE NOW SEE THESE TWO PEOPLE AT THE SAME TIME ON A SPLIT SCREEN.) In each of these last two cases both characters will be 'shot' separately and the resulting images will be 'mixed' in an editing suite later.

I personally don't like to see the split-screen method used. I feel it gives an even more artificial quality to something that's artificial to begin with and which you're trying to make seem 'real', and I never use it. The third option – moving from one character and location to the other and back again – is the one I prefer to see, but you can make your own choice.

The good news is that, if you prefer flitting from scene to scene, as I do, you should never need to write a simple exchange of dialogue that requires ten or more scene headings. The not-quite-so-good news is that, if you do it as described above, you will have to rely on the director to choose the shots he or she prefers – rather than the precise ones you might have specified if you had described *every* change of scene yourself. You can, however, nudge the director in the 'right' direction by mentioning a visual or two such as: (JACK LOOKS UPSET AS HE HEARS THIS) or by describing the fact that someone else has entered one room or the other, so the director will understand we need to see this.

Make a note

- Establishing shots can be useful and not too expensive.
- They can bridge the gap between one interior scene and another.
- They can be used to set the general locations in an opening sequence.
- Each establishing shot will count as a separate scene and be written as such.
- Phone conversations need special attention and can be played in four different ways. It can help to vary these, but not within the same conversation.

The Dynamics of a Scene

Having just mentioned the kind of scene (the establishing shot) where nothing much happens, perhaps this is as good a place as any to talk about scenes where something definitely *does* happen.

Most, if not all, scenes should be there for a reason other than to fill the gap between one 'important' scene and another. Something should be said or done that *adds* to what we already know. A scene, however brief, should either push the story along – delineate character, give more information, imply something in the subtext – or simply amuse us. In other words it should do at least one or two of those things we talked about regarding dialogue.

Now that scenes have become shorter and faster this no

longer strictly applies. There are definitely scenes now that just bridge the gaps and make the piece as a whole flow more realistically. Two people having a deeply interesting conversation might move from the bedroom to the kitchen, then to the lounge, then to the back garden and then back again just to make a sequence appear less static. This can turn what would have been one scene a few years ago into half a dozen or more, and in terms of drama it's hard to see any great value. But the people who make the shows and the majority of viewers seem to prefer it that way, so it's as well to go along with the general trend at the moment.

Things may change back again and certain shows that have been successful in recent years – like *The Royle Family* and to a lesser extent *The Office* – seem to prove that scenes lasting more than sixty seconds don't always leave the viewer sighing with boredom.

So what can we say about a single scene that would be helpful to a new writer? More or less what's already been said in the exercise about duologues. A scene should have a beginning, a middle and an end, just like the story itself but in miniature. It should start with some kind of premise, move on to a complication and some kind of mini-climax, and end with a resolution but not a *final* one – just one that promises more to come. In other words something should have *happened* in that minute or two – maybe just a change of attitude by one person towards another, or some kind of decision agreed upon, however trivial. It should fit into the overall scheme of things like a single piece fits snugly into a jigsaw puzzle. And there should be a focus on one character or another so that we are seeing things from his or her point of view. There should be one character 'driving' the scene (again – just as we saw in the duologue).

You, as writer, have to make it clear that you aren't simply standing back and *describing* a series of things as they happen to a bunch of people who are strangers to you. You are right in there *living* it, sometimes as one character and sometimes as another, and you decide who you are at any particular moment by deciding who is the pivotal character in that scene.

In a thirty-minute piece it's quite possible that your main character will be the pivotal character in most of the scenes, but there will probably be some scenes in which he or she *doesn't* appear. Those scenes will still need a pivotal character for you to focus on and through. It shouldn't be a difficult decision for you to make, and usually you'll find yourself doing it automatically, but just in case this doesn't happen make the decision consciously. Think to yourself, 'Who is driving this scene? Which character are we following at this particular moment?' You'll find that even though these distinctions can be quite subtle they are still important, and scenes that don't have a pivotal character can help to make the story as a whole lose direction. It's like the exercise on a change of pivotal character that you were asked to do earlier. Switch the focus and you can change the direction of the story completely.

Imagine, for instance, a fairly simple family scene where a daughter is telling her impoverished parents that she wants to leave university and get a job in a supermarket where she can start earning money straight away. From the daughter's point of view this could be an act of sacrifice, something she regrets having to do but which she's prepared to do out of loyalty.

From the mother's point of view it could bring a mixture of relief and sadness. She feels grateful to her daughter for helping out in a desperate situation, but sorrow that it's had to come to this.

The father, on the other hand, might feel devastated and see it as a profound failure on his part. He could leave this encounter feeling suicidal.

You could choose to focus on any one of these three people with very different results. Suppose your vehicle story was about the daughter, in a 'triumph over adversity' type story where she eventually bcomes manageress of the supermarket and finds herself employing people with university degrees. Then we might still follow her father enough to see him taking an overdose, but we'd be doing that not as an end to itself, but as a way of seeing how it affected the daughter. She would *still* be the pivotal character in the single scene we've discussed and in the drama as a whole. The story wouldn't end with the father's attempted suicide, it would end with the daughter's triumph and possibly the father's recovery.

It's not a matter of absolutes. We wouldn't say that this is the daughter's story, not the father's. It's just a matter of emphasis, so we'd say that this is *more* the daughter's story than the father's. And of course, whoever's story it is, it would still include the others but to a slightly lesser degree.

Make a note

- Some short scenes are there to add visual interest and help the flow.
- Most scenes have a pivotal character.
- A good scene should have a beginning, middle and end.
- Scenes should be *lived out* and written from 'within', not just *described.*

By now you should have learned enough to start thinking about making a start on the real thing.

Part Two
Taking the Plunge

7 Method Over Madness

One-minute Overview

In this chapter you'll be preparing to make a start on the real thing by taking a professional approach to the task ahead. You'll be shown a detailed plan of how to set about it and a timetable to help you maintain a suitable focus. You'll be told what I firmly believe to be the most efficient way to work and also what I've found throughout my teaching career, with large numbers of students, to be the least efficient way to work. The choice will be yours.

Taking Aim

To write any kind of script with no particular target in mind is a bit like walking into a field at random and shooting an arrow into the sky on the off chance that there might be an archery target somewhere just out of sight. The chances would be slim and even if you had, by sheer good luck, happened to choose a field belonging to the local Robin Hood Preservation Society, the chances of your scoring a bulls-eye wouldn't be very great.

It's surprising how many new writers ignore the fairly obvious demands of the marketplace and persist in writing whatever *they* want to write. That's admirable in some ways, because without innovation any creative activity would eventually lose its appeal for all concerned. But unless you have a really exceptional talent, or perhaps 'death wish' would be another way of putting it, it's as well to settle for a compromise. If you're aiming a script at the BBC or any British TV company it should fit some sort of current time-slot and probably be set in Britain. (I'm thinking ahead now to a time *after* you've written your thirty-minute calling-card script, and want to use the skills you've been sharpening to try for something more adventurous.) For the moment, however, let's get back to the business in hand. If you've bought this book and read this far then you already have your general aim, which is to write a thirty-minute script that might get you noticed. However, you still need to refine your target. Are you happy to write a straight drama that has little chance of being considered as a one-off project (as I explained earlier in the book, there are very few slots available for thirty-minute one-off shows at the moment) or do you fancy writing your calling-card script as a sitcom pilot?

The decision is up to you, but I have to tell you at this point that a sitcom pilot will need another five storylines to back it up. It will be no good sending one script that impresses somebody and then admitting you hadn't thought what might happen in Episode Two. Just bear that in mind (and more will be said about it later). At the moment you have to decide *exactly* what kind of calling-card script you want to write with regard to genre and tone.

Is it going to be a simple domestic drama involving relationships, a ghost or horror story, a murder mystery, a piece of fantasy or science fiction, or some kind of one-off comedy drama? I've already advised you to keep it simple and uncluttered, so maybe you already know what you have in mind. If not, now is the time to give it serious thought.

Think also about the soap or drama series you would most like to write for. How close in style, without being a parody or rip-off, would *your* idea come to this? Can you imagine the producers of *Eastenders* or *Doctors*, both very realistic and down-to-earth shows, being suitably impressed by a script about robots from outer space invading the planet?

Maybe they would. They might see it as a nice change, and you could certainly use such a script to show that you've learned some of the necessary skills – even if you're showing them in a different way. But you decide for yourself.

Start with a Plan

One of the first questions my students ask me is: how do you actually make a start on a script? Is there some sort of formula to follow? Well, I'm sure many writers have a different approach from my own. Some will literally start writing the dialogue with a couple of characters they know very little about (as you did with the first exercise in this book) and let it flow from there. Others will mull over an idea for months, if not years, before sketching out the overall scheme on a scrap of paper. I have one friend who writes key moments on pieces of card, using different coloured card for the main plot and the sub-plots, and then assembles them a bit like a jigsaw.

Whatever works best for you is the method to follow eventually, and there's no reason at all why you shouldn't devise your own way of doing things. But you have to start somewhere and I have a method, a kind of 'painting by numbers' approach, that I discovered by trial and error and which I've stuck to ever since.

It might not seem, at first glance, to be the most creative way but I find it the most efficient and the amount of creativity you use once you get into the flow is up to you. I know this method works because I explain it to my university students and the people attending my writing workshops, and with my guidance most of them manage to write a complete script in ten weeks.

Here is something I give to all my students near the halfway point in their course. (It's slightly modified here because I deliberately leave some things 'open' for my students, to invite discussion, and I won't get that chance with you.) I explain to them in person, just as I'm explaining to you in print, that they won't understand everything at first glance. Things will become much more clear as you learn through experience and as more details are given later. Just stick with it and have some trust in the fact that I've been doing this kind of thing for a long time now and I know that it works.

Here's my plan:

Method plan

1. Get an **initial idea** and choose something you either know a lot about or are very interested in, in terms of genre/style/location/characters. Keep the *main* characters to a minimum – four to six is plenty for a new writer. Don't make life hard for yourself.

2. Spend a few hours turning this idea into a **one-page outline** with the five-step basic story shape in mind. And as a reminder, here are those five steps again:
   a) Introduce main character/characters and set location, style, genre.
   b) Provide 'hook' very quickly.
   c) Introduce complications.
   d) Short exciting/dramatic climax.
   e) Resolution.

   This one-page outline can be as detailed or as sketchy as you like so long as you have a beginning, a middle and an end, and a route to follow that you know can work on a basic level.

   Your plan will probably undergo many changes, but the important thing is that you can press on with confidence, knowing you have a definite route to follow. Think of yourself as an explorer, but one guided by a map, however imperfect, and with the certain knowledge that the place being sought really does exist.

3. Now you're ready to start thinking of your idea in script terms. So turn your one-page outline into a simple **basic step outline** containing twelve to fifteen scenes but still using prose to describe what happens – not script format or direct speech (dialogue). And only write one or two sentences for each scene. I'd advise you to limit your interior sets to about six, including a multiple set of maybe three rooms, and your exterior locations to between three and six. So that's a maximum of twelve different scene settings in total. It's not always necessary to set your scenes out chronologically at first. It can be helpful to jump from the opening to the end before filling in the gaps, something like this.

   Scene 1
   You think of a suitably dramatic and engaging way to introduce the main characters/set location/genre/tone. (Immediately – no time wasted on lengthy introductions.) Then move on to ...

   Scene 2
   This is where you provide the 'hook' (let the reader know what the problem or task, the central premise, is going to be). Then, instead of going on to Scene 3 you jump ahead to ...

   Scenes 12–15
   These will incorporate the climax and the resolution.

   So now you can be sure you have a strong beginning and a strong ending. You can happily go back and fill in the gaps with *main* developments – as I've already said, just one or two sentences for each scene. That leaves you with a completed **basic step outline**, and you can play around with it a little if you like. Now is the best time to do this before you start adding more details.

4. Write brief biographies for each of your main characters. Just a few paragraphs on each one will do, and maybe it's best to limit this to just three or four of your characters in a thirty-minute piece – don't risk losing focus.

5. Then you do a more **detailed step outline**, adding extra scenes where appropriate. Be aware that many thirty-minute TV pieces nowadays will have anything from twenty to forty scenes.

6. After this you do the **completed first draft** but with **improvised dialogue.** That is just getting the points across quickly without paying too much attention to accents, witty remarks or subtext – just finish it in a creative rush.

7. Now look back over it and **re-shape** where necessary. Check the need for sub-plots if it's too 'thin', and make sure more than one character has worked out their agenda and 'developed' by the end.

8. Now rewrite the dialogue for the **penultimate draft** using the **five functions of dialogue**, mentioned earlier in the book, as a check-list. Remember what was said about these rules: 'good' dialogue should always be doing at least one of the things mentioned in this list. As a reminder, here they are again:
   a) Push the story along.
   b) Give necessary information.
   c) Delineate character.
   d) Have a subtext.
   e) Set up or pay off a funny line.

9. Ask friends or family to do a read-through of your script whilst you watch and take notes. Don't expect people to read a script 'cold' without having a

chance to read it silently first. Encourage them to ask questions about things they don't understand, or about the character they are being asked to portray.

Once they've started the actual read-through together try not to interrupt too much – just let it flow. You can read the stage directions if necessary because this will help everyone to visualise the parts without dialogue and it should make the timing of the piece more accurate. After this you can ask for comments again. Generally I advise students to pay close attention if several people all make the same criticism but to trust their own judgement when people disagree. Of course, you must trust your own judgement anyway.

10. Now, having taken on board any suggestions you agree with, rewrite it for the **final draft**.

And that's it. My own preferred way of doing things.

The Most Efficient Way To Do It

The method described above is only one way of doing it but it's a way that *works*. It's so much easier to start with the skeleton first, then add the flesh, then the fine details. Bearing this analogy in mind, just imagine the mess you would make by doing it the other way around. Or, to use a less graphic analogy, imagine setting off on a marathon race without first checking for directions, then discovering after twenty miles or so that you had set off in completely the wrong direction.

The Least Efficient Way To Do It

I don't favour jumping right in and writing the dialogue early (except for practice sessions that are nothing to do with your actual script), because if you write dialogue that's 'good', witty, telling or poetic, then you'll fight to keep it even when it no longer fits, and you'll waste time doing this – sometimes a lot of time.

If you start with the idea first it's easy to change it completely: give it a new ending, change the pivotal character or change the whole theme, and you can do this in minutes. But if you've started to create 'real' characters too early and grown to like them you can easily get confused by the welter of details even the simplest change will bring, and spend days changing things you needn't have written in the first place.

Setting a Time Limit

If you really are aiming to do the whole process in ten weeks then I'd advise you to do it my way first and time the stages something like this:

Weeks One/Four Read the whole book. Absorb some of the information given and do the exercises. Then go back to Chapter Seven and start reading again as you write your script.

Week Five One-page outline completed, with a good beginning, middle and end. Know what happens and why (story and theme). Produce basic step outline of ten to fifteen scenes described briefly in prose.

Week Five/Six	Write brief biographies for main characters (just three or four of them). Then write out a twenty-to-forty scene *detailed* step outline (still in prose – not as a TV script and with little if any actual dialogue – just reported speech, e.g. 'Nigel tells his wife he's leaving her').
Weeks Six/Eight	Write first draft, in script form and with *improvised* dialogue (not carefully crafted dialogue at this point).
Week Eight/Nine	Write second draft and now personalise the dialogue to fit the characters better. Make sure it does at least *some* of the other things mentioned in the five functions of dialogue (use the five rules as a checklist).
Week Nine/Ten	Hold the script read-through with friends or family and do the final rewrites.

Don't worry at all if your own schedule works out very differently from this. You may get so fired up that you complete the first step in a single day rather than a week. That's fine – you'll have more time left for the rest of it. But if it takes you *longer* than a week, who cares? Nobody's given you a tight deadline. Remember what I said about juggling? It's the end product that counts at this stage in your development and just like in the old fable, slow and steady can win the race.

If you do manage to follow this plan, however roughly, you will have completed your first TV script in ten weeks as promised, and even if it's not yet good enough to submit you will have learned a lot in the process. You should feel like a person who's just passed their driving test – ready to drive on your own, if not quite ready to win a Grand Prix.

You can then either send out the script and see what responses you get or put it to one side and start all over again, using the above method once more or trying a different approach if preferred. Bear in mind that this is a very competitive market you're aiming at and that TV scriptwriting is a craft as well as an art – and crafts have to be practised.

Create Your First Real One-page Story Outline

Look again at the beginning of the method plan. Read what it says about starting with a basic idea that you either know a lot about or are very interested in, in terms of genre/style/location/characters.

Keep the *main* characters to a minimum – four to six is plenty for a new writer. Don't make life hard for yourself.

Make sure you start with a pivotal character and start to tell the story in such a way that the reader, and later the viewer, will identify with this central character and care about him or her. Without this 'angle' you won't be telling a story, you'll be describing a series of events. You're trying to write a TV drama or comedy, not make suggestions for a documentary.

So, if you haven't already done so, decide right now what kind of story you want to tell, in terms of genre and style: a hard-hitting story about life as a drug squad officer, a romantic comedy about an impoverished young man falling in love with a sophisticated older woman, or whatever.

Decide where it's going to take place – London, Manchester, Liverpool or wherever (somewhere you know about or think is the most suitable place). Decide which character is the pivotal one (or viewpoint character) and start with their name – something like this: 'James Colbourne has been working as a drug squad officer in Nottingham for ten years. He's forty-five years old and beginning to look older. The strains of the job and his fondness for a drink have helped to end what was a happy marriage. James isn't such a bad guy – he's honest and decent but perhaps over-committed to his work. He takes things personally, as if it's his job alone to keep the back streets of the city "clean" and drug free. He doesn't see the irony of his own drinking and smoking.'

I just wrote the first name that came into my head and took it from there. I have no intention of finishing this outline, but if I did it might carry on to say that James suddenly finds himself investigating his own teenage son, who's become involved with a gang of drug-dealers. Perhaps this quickly escalates into a suspected murder case? Maybe James finds himself in a position where he could lie to help his son, and the story becomes a test of his integrity – especially if his estranged wife knows what's going on and pleads with James to help. She says that their marriage could be saved if James is prepared, at long last, to show he really does care more for his family than his job. And of course James would already be feeling guilty, knowing that his own failure to keep the marriage alive was partly to blame for his son's behaviour ...

You can see how the story could develop in various different ways. James might lie to help his son and be found out. He might lie at first, then realise his son really was the murderer and someone else was about to get the blame. Or he might realise that his estranged wife was the murderer and the murdered man had been her lover *and* the person who'd introduced the son to drugs. It's a bit far-fetched but not impossible, and in fact there could be any number of different twists and turns.

Then you decide what kind of ending you want – happy or sad or somewhere in between. Having made that decision you then determine what the theme of it all is (only on a general level – don't get bogged down trying to be too analytical). Do you want to say that it pays to be honest – or perhaps warn that honesty has a price? Do you want to say that loyalty to the family should come before anything else or that you ignore moral standards at your peril? Do you want to say that there is always hope – or that society is going to the dogs? Having made that decision, your ending should more or less write itself.

Bear in mind that, although you may have been focusing on one main character, you've also mentioned other characters, and any one of these characters can provide a sub-plot if your story needs it. Just make sure the sub-plot not only interweaves with the main plot but also reflects on it in some way. The story sketched out above could easily have a sub-plot involving James's wife and her lover, or James's son and the problems he discusses with his girlfriend in a relationship that seems to mirror that of his parents.

Make sure you have a really solid main plot first, and even when you introduce a sub-plot make sure it doesn't unbalance the main plot. You can easily add a sub-plot at a later stage, but it's harder to rescue a main plot that's been swamped by too many diversions.

Don't forget to look again at the classic story shape. Here it is again in brief:

1. Introduce main character/s and set tone and general location.
2. Provide hook.
3. Complications.

4. Climax.

5. Resolution.

At this stage you can happily spend a few hours or days thinking about this kind of thing. It's fun and not that draining. Try to make sure you're reasonably happy with your one-page outline, and particularly your main plot, before you move on.

Make a note

- Take careful aim.
- Start with a plan and follow it.
- Try to stick to some sort of timetable, however flexible.
- Begin your story outline with the pivotal character to engage the audience.
- Make sure you have a beginning, middle and end that 'work' before moving on.
- Be more concerned with the main plot than sub-plots at this stage.
- Understand that nothing is set in stone and things can change if necessary.

8 Up Close and Personal

One-minute Overview

In this chapter you will focus more on the details of structure: of making your script not just look professional but also have the depth and quality of a script worth taking seriously. You'll be told why many new scripts get rejected almost at first glance and how to avoid this. You'll learn how to vary scenes and how to use sub-plots effectively. You'll be advised what to do when you feel 'stuck' at any time and feel like giving up. More will be said about the opening sequence and about how to 'signpost' future developments so that things don't just happen out of the blue and fail to convince. Symbolism gets a brief mention, and you'll be shown how to turn a one-page outline into a basic step outline for a TV script. More will be said about how character biographies can help with storylines and then you'll be shown how to turn your basic step outline into a more detailed one.

Why Most New Scripts are Rejected

It's a mistake to think that scripts are turned down for not quite reaching the required standards. The truth is that many scripts by new writers are well wide of the mark and an experienced script-editor or producer will only have to skim through the script and perhaps read the first two or three pages to make a decision about it.

Many don't even look professional. They aren't set out in any recognised format, and a quick glance through the pages shows that scene changes aren't indicated properly and that the scenes themselves are often too long and static. The dialogue is often set out in regular chunks, more like stage dialogue than TV dialogue. TV dialogue usually has shorter speeches that are often interrupted and appear less tidy on the page. So someone who's made the effort to read a book like this and learn about correct layout and more appropriate dialogue starts with a distinct advantage.

Although many would-be scriptwriters are naturally good at creating characters and writing 'witty' dialogue, the things that *don't* come naturally are the real give-aways. The technicalities, like layout and scene changes, can be learned quite quickly but the really difficult thing is structure. knowing how much information to give at any one time, knowing when to leave one strand of development and follow another, or how to vary the pace and tone of scenes to avoid monotony. These can all be learned as well but need a lot of practice.

Sharpening your appreciation of dialogue and understanding why people react to one another in certain ways can be absorbed all the time. You just need to be aware of what's going on around you. You can listen and observe.

Learning about *structure* isn't so easy, because real life is all too random and complicated. It isn't structured, in the way that a drama needs to be if it's going to hold the attention for even thirty minutes, and that's something you can't simply observe. You have to take the raw material and shape it just as a sculptor might take a pile of clay and turn it into a work of art.

The Vital Importance of Structure

It's usually lack of structure and technique that shows the real difference between an amateur, however naturally gifted, and a trained professional. It's as simple as that.

Pay a lot of attention to the structure of your script before adding the details with dialogue and precise visuals.

How You Can Vary Scenes

As already mentioned in an earlier chapter, one way to make a script seem tired and static is to have scenes that are too similar following one after another. This has a kind of subconscious hypnotic effect on the brain – perhaps even lulling viewers to sleep.

Obviously the thing to do is vary the scenes. Aside from those things already mentioned, they can be varied in terms of:

Location	From interior to exterior and vice-versa.
Length	Short scene – longer scene – medium scene, and so on.
Content	Noisy argumentative scene – quiet reflective scene.
Action	Busy physical scene – quiet, intimate scene.
Numbers	Large cast scene – small cast scene.
Tone	Funny scene – deadly serious scene.
Sound/vision	Lots of dialogue – purely visual (no dialogue at all).
Establishing shot	Simple 'still' shot that remains the same no matter how many times it's shown – simple 'moving' shot (character approaching building etc).

Of course these guidelines mustn't be followed too strictly or in too regimented a fashion, or that in itself will cause a regularity that could become tedious. It's a case of mix and match. You look at your script and realise you have three duologues all following one another, all lasting sixty seconds, all indoors and all of a similar tone. In that case it's definitely time to add variety. If your script seems to bounce along quite naturally don't start changing it just for the sake of adding more variety. If you have a really long scene that seems to work – leave it alone. It's all a matter of judgement – it's not mathematics.

Sub-plots

Many new writers are frightened by the thought of having more than one plot to fit into their drama, but it isn't always as complicated or difficult as it might seem.

If you have worked out a main plot and created realistic characters to act it out then it's almost impossible to avoid having a few sub-plots, or at least the basis to build them on. It's fairly simple. Your main character won't be working in a vacuum. He or she will be interacting with other characters all the time. And at least a few of these characters should be fully rounded enough to be considered as real people. Real people *always* have something happening in their lives. You just have to make sure you only include things that enhance your drama as a whole and fit in with the main story.

Perhaps it's as well to remember *theme* here. Don't try to show two or more conflicting themes. If your general theme is about the dangers of being unfaithful make sure a secondary character doesn't seem to prove the opposite – by getting away with something and being happy about it. He or she can be happy of course – but by being *faithful* and doing the 'right' thing. This won't confuse your aims but will strengthen them.

A main plot about a man planning to leave his wife and children for a younger woman will obviously not only be about the man himself. It will also be about his wife, his children and the other woman. It might also involve his parents, his best friend or his boss at work. And all these other people will have an attitude towards what's happening.

All you have to do is decide which of these characters can provide the most mileage in terms of a sub-plot, or secondary story. Then spend some time weaving *that* story in and out of the main one, making sure you don't get confused about which is which.

Suppose you choose the wife and the man's best friend as the two most promising sub-plot characters. Maybe these two characters once hated each other but become close friends who now start supporting each other. They might then fall in love, or simply give each other the confidence to make important decisions. And maybe we also realise that the husband isn't getting such a good bargain anyway, as his girlfriend is already making demands as they drive off into a sunset that promises to be more of a downpour.

Or suppose you chose the man's father as a suitable sub-plot character. Maybe he's always spoiled his son and given him everything he ever asked for. Maybe he too had affairs and treated the main character's mother badly, showing little respect and therefore being a bad role model. Then some of your drama could be taken up with the sub-plot of the parent's relationship. Maybe the day the main character leaves his wife is the day his mother plucks up the courage to leave his father? It's true that this wouldn't be a very happy ending, but it could be a meaningful one as the mother exhorts her daughter-in-law not to waste the rest of her life pining for a man who was a spoilt brat anyway, but to be brave and hope for something better in the future. And maybe the mother would promise to help by being a better support than she had ever been before.

So you can see from these brief examples how relatively easy it is to come up with sub-plots. There are so many possibilities that the real danger is you'll find too many and over-complicate your drama.

You can avoid that by remembering a few simple rules. Always start your main plot first and end it last. That gives it the importance you want, and of course will mean that it's the *longest* plot. Start your most important sub-plot shortly *after* you've set the main plot in motion, but end it shortly *before* you finish the main one. This obviously makes it shorter. Follow this simple rule for any third sub-plot. Start it in third place, but finish it *before* both the others.

I wouldn't advise any more than two sub-plots in a thirty-minute piece and I'd urge you to keep the second sub-plot, in particular, quite slight – perhaps not even a story in itself but just a change of attitude on the part of that character. For example, a man's boss decides to give someone else the promotion the man was expecting. In all cases, in a thirty-minute piece, make sure the sub-plots really do impinge upon the main plot in an interesting way that supports the main theme rather than weakens it.

Writer's Block

I tell my students there is really no such thing as writer's block. (Okay, so maybe I lie to them a little bit – maybe there *is* such a thing and it's recognised by psychologists or clever people in general, but I don't want to know that.) I tell my students that saying you have writer's block is really like saying you can't be bothered – can't be bothered to make a start, at least, and risk getting it wrong before you get it right.

I tell them that I had many jobs before I became a teacher and then a writer. I once worked, for example, for a small company that cleaned all the windows at the various Rolls-Royce factory sites in Derby. The work was physically demanding and sometimes dangerous – not quite as straightforward as you might imagine. Where and how you placed a massive ladder, in a crowded car park or on a strip of wet grass, could require a certain amount of skill and caution. But I never once complained, and nor did any of my colleagues, that we were suffering from window-cleaner's block. The condition just didn't exist.

We didn't stand around wondering if we ought to clean the windows in a circular motion or in straight lines going from corner to corner. We just climbed up the ladder and got on with it. By and large this seemed to work quite well and we rarely missed a deadline. If it started to pour with rain we would stop what we were doing and move inside the factory to clean the inside of the panes; when it stopped raining we would go outside again.

You can take the same attitude with regard to your writing. Sit down at your desk and make a start. If you don't feel like using your computer, write in your notepad. You'll find this nearly always works. Once you actually make a start your creative mind slips into gear and you're away. It doesn't matter if you write rubbish at first – nobody is going to see it.

Robert McKee feels much the same as I do about this. At one of his lectures I heard him talk about a little child who has fallen down and grazed his knee. The child won't sit on the floor thinking of the best way to describe this to somebody. He will let out a yell, go rushing to his mother or father and say, 'I've hurt my knee.' The 'right' words will just come out automatically. He has something to say and he'll get the message across very effectively without even thinking about it.

McKee seems to be suggesting that writer's block really means, 'I've got nothing to say,' so make sure you *have* got something to say and get on with it.

Starting with an Earthquake

Remember the Hollywood producer who supposedly said to a writer, 'I want you to start this picture with an earthquake and then build up to an exciting climax'? True or not, it's an engaging little anecdote and perhaps even more telling in these days of high-tech graphics and all-action movies like *The Lord of the Rings.* It might even be good advice for a film script writer, but for anyone trying to write a thirty-minute TV script it can be safely ignored.

Yes, by all means start off with an arresting incident that helps provide a good hook. An episode of *Clocking Off*, the drama series written by Paul Abbott and shown on BBC 1, opened on a shot of two clowns running breathlessly down a street in the middle of the night after setting fire to a suburban semi. It was pretty riveting stuff and the scenes that followed, of one of the 'clowns' realising that her own mother and children were trapped inside the house, and then of a neighbour desperately trying to rescue one of the children, kept up this intense level of tension for several minutes.

The writer was helped by excellent direction and camera work. A fairly ordinary semi suddenly looked like a skyscraper when filmed from a low angle. The man using a ladder to bridge the gap between his own upstairs window and the one in the burning house looked like someone doing a dangerous high-wire act. It seemed that he only had to fall to be dashed to pieces on the ground far below and he acted with appropriate caution. All I can say is that he would never have got a job with the window cleaning company that had the contract with Rolls Royce. It's true that we didn't usually clean windows with flames roaring out of them, but we were happy to go higher than the fifteen feet or so that marks the bottom of a bedroom window in the average suburban semi.

Having said all that, I would defy anyone to watch this opening sequence and not bother to find out what it was all about. Why were the two characters dressed as clowns? Why had they set fire to the house in the first place? And so on. This opening didn't just provide one excellent hook – it had several.

If you care to analyse this particular episode, however, you'll realise that the writer got away with some pretty impressive artistic licence. It turned out that one of the characters dressed as clowns, the one who had torched her own house, had done it for the insurance money. Now just stop and think of the logic involved here. You've decided to torch your own house, so you think: 'Oh, I know. I'll do it on the night of the firm's fancy-dress ball, dressed as a clown.' Why would anyone do that? (Except to provide a colourful and intriguing opening to a TV drama?)

In reality you would surely do it in the most unobtrusive way possible, knowing that someone is bound to investigate later. Imagine the police or some insurance investigator asking questions of the neighbours. 'Did you notice anything suspicious?' 'No, not really. Oh, except for these two clowns who seemed to be very upset about it all.' 'And did you have any idea where the woman who owns the house was at the time?' 'I'm not sure, but I think she was at a fancy-dress party.'

Hmm – very dodgy. But Paul Abbott not only got away with it, he turned it into a triumph. I wouldn't be too sure that many new writers could do the same. So what I would advise, in general, is that you *don't* start with an earthquake and try to build up to an exciting climax. You start with something suitably arresting, but something you can definitely build on. It might be as simple as a person receiving a phone call we don't even hear but which makes the character appear tense. Then the viewer will wonder if he or she has had bad news from a hospital, an ex-partner or a blackmailer, maybe. And then you can start raising the stakes as mentioned in Chapter Three. Even something serious like a person being sacked or suffering the death of a partner isn't quite the same as an earthquake. These are still things that can get worse before getting better.

While I'm talking about beginnings again this might be a good place to say: don't try to introduce too many characters at once. Introduce your main character and just one or two others at the beginning of a thirty-minute piece. Other main characters can then be gradually introduced a scene or two later. As a new writer, try to avoid having five or six important characters all making their first appearance at the same time, particularly right at the beginning when the viewer or script-reader will be trying to sort out exactly what is going on.

Make life easy for yourself – and for others.

Signposting

This is another thing you don't always need to think about consciously as you write the script. As you become more experienced it will come naturally and you will automatically start to mention relevant things that you know will feature later. But often it's only when you get further into your script that you'll realise you've suddenly introduced a person, an object or a situation that seems to have arrived out of the blue and isn't very convincing. It needed to be mentioned earlier (signposting), and you can go back and do that quite easily.

Let me make up a brief example of this. Suppose you've written one of those currently popular maniac-at-loose-in-the-house plays. You know the type of thing I mean. A woman takes on a full-time female nurse to help care for her elderly father and the woman seems perfect at first. But then she starts doing little things that don't seem quite right: opening and answering the elderly man's mail, sending his name to a dating agency and then pretending to *be* him by wearing one of his suits and smoking a pipe to interview potential suitors. And by the end of the drama the crazy nurse has tied the man up in the kitchen and is chasing the woman through the house with an axe.

Now, if the woman being chased suddenly runs into an attic room, lifts up a loose floorboard and takes out a loaded revolver, just as the crazy woman is using the axe to smash through the door, it will come as a surprise and a not-very-convincing one. Now go back through your script, perhaps to the very beginning where the main character finds her elderly father looking at a pistol he brought back from the Second World War as a souvenir. She thinks he might be thinking of suicide and takes the gun away from him, promising not to throw it away but to keep it somewhere safe. Thus we not only signpost the gun and where it is, but also supply a reason for the daughter to hire a nurse in the first place. On top of which we have a pretty good opening sequence with a good hook. The old man might be going crazy and there's a gun in the house.

As a bonus it might work well if we don't let the audience know that the gun is actually loaded. There's no reason why the daughter should know that either. Maybe she could ask her father and he makes a sarcastic remark about her thinking he's crazy. So now when the woman runs into the attic room the audience will know why she's done that, but will still be scared because they think the gun isn't loaded. Then the crazy woman could be stopped in her tracks at the sight of the gun, but rush back to the kitchen where she can kill the old man or hold him hostage. And just as she's about to finish him off she's shot by the gun we thought wasn't loaded, and maybe that makes the old man realise that his memory is going and he really does need help. So we will not only have re-incorporated the gun but also what the old man said about it.

Anyway – you can see how signposting isn't just a necessary function but something that can add to and improve your script.

Symbolism

This is something that seems a bit neglected in modern TV drama, and perhaps today's quick-moving scenes make inner reflection difficult. In fact, symbolism has always been a contentious issue and it's easy to see things in a drama that the writer probably never intended us to see or, paradoxically, to completely miss things that *were* intended.

One of the first things I wrote as a professional was a play called *King of The Blues*, which was about a star footballer who received so much adulation that he began to imagine he might really be a reincarnation of Jesus. I thought the title itself was a very obvious symbolic link. Perhaps too obvious – *King of the Blues*, instead of King of the Jews. And I was quite surprised to realise that many people hadn't made this connection at all and thought the title meant exactly what it said. The player was a star for Birmingham City, a team nicknamed The Blues.

I made countless links with parts of the Bible. For instance, the star player befriends a prostitute (and on second thoughts that one was perhaps open to misinterpretation). But we also had the footballer telling anecdotes to his team-mates, such as the parable of the central defender which ended with God in his infinite wisdom saying, 'That's the way the ball bounces.' And we also had the main character, Mark Neal, trying to feed five thousand people, at a meeting between fans and management – and failing, since the chip shop was closed. We showed betrayal and temptation and ended up with a pitch invasion during which Mark was spreadeagled by rioting 'fans' and stabbed to death.

In fact, the story of the football star mirrored the last days of Jesus very closely, but generally people just wanted to laugh at the jokes and the whole play was 'sold' as a comedy about football, which wasn't what I'd intended at all.

On another occasion, when I was much younger, I remember taking a girlfriend to see *Dr Zhivago*, in which there's a scene (if memory serves me right) where a glass of red wine is spilled on a young virgin's beautiful white dress. Even in those days I was deeply into analysing films and dramas so I leaned closer to my girlfriend and whispered confidently, 'Hmm. You know what that means, don't you?' 'Yes,' she replied. 'They'll waste some of the white wine trying to get that stain out.' I'm still not sure if she was joking, but when I told her what I thought it meant she sighed and said, 'You've just got a dirty mind.'

More recently, I was impressed with some of the scenes from a film called *Stepping Out*, which I can heartily recommend you watch out for as a re-run on TV or buy on dvd. It has some excellent examples of duologues and of 'talky' scenes in general, using great dialogue. It also has a wonderful theme of triumph over adversity, as shown through the lives of several of the characters, and interweaves the various stories in a very satisfying structure.

It isn't perfect. The scenes involving the relationship between the main character, played by Liza Minnelli, and her male partner seemed underdeveloped and sometimes murkily shot – and perhaps this is an example of symbolism that is irritating rather than effective. But there are several moments of pure symbolic joy. The one that sticks out most in my mind occurs as Liza, playing the part of a dance teacher, is sitting in the church hall she uses as a studio. (That setting may be a symbol in itself, though it's not unusual in the circumstances.)

She's trying to work out a routine for her pupils, who have been invited to take part in a show, and she's determined to get it right because, amongst other things, the snotty woman who's organising the show has been really patronising to her and, by implication, her pupils. As the character Liza plays is feeling worried and frustrated, a shaft of sunlight shines through a high window and hits her like a stage spotlight. Without a word being spoken we know immediately that this reminds her of the time when she appeared on stage as a professional. She dances to the taped music (quite brilliantly) and the story is given a massive boost as we know she is never going to give up until her students have given their all. At the end of the dance she is framed by a huge stained-glass window in such a way that she almost becomes part of it.

It's very theatrical and symbolic at the same time. Where better to find a symbol of hope than in a stained-glass window? Get the dvd and watch it for yourself. It should inspire you.

Obvious uses of symbolism are thunder and lightning on a dark night to promote terror, rainfall to dampen someone's enthusiasm, sunshine to suggest optimism and snowfall to suggest nostalgia and innocence – a return to childhood. The weather is something that can be used without too much difficulty or confusion, although it isn't always easy to guarantee real snow in large quantities.

In general I'd advise you not to spend too much time searching for subtle symbols. Sadly, it's quite likely that few people will notice them anyway, but on the other hand if *you* are interested in using them then why not go for it? It's hard to see it doing any harm. Just don't be too surprised if you show your main character looking thoughtfully at a pair of tap shoes and musing on the distant days when he dreamed of becoming the next Gene Kelly, and the audience merely think he's a foot fetishist or that he's thinking of becoming a cobbler.

Turning a One-page Outline into a Basic Step Outline

You will by now have your one-page outline ready. It might help here if I give a very simple example of how turning that into a basic step outline works. To do that I could use an example from one of my own TV scripts, but I thought it might be more fun to use a less complex idea that you are probably already familiar with.

Each year for the past ten years I've written a panto script for the children in the church I attend to perform at Christmas. The panto is for very young children, so thirty minutes is long enough, which makes it suitable for this exercise even though it's for stage not screen. I hope you'll see what I mean.

I start by doing a one-page outline of the story I want to adapt. Let's take *Rumpelstiltskin*, because despite its twists and turns it's a pretty straightforward storyline and one that most of you will already know. It also has just about the right number of speaking characters for us to deal with to mirror your attempt to write an uncluttered calling-card script. (Remember, just four to six main characters are plenty.)

Please don't skip over this story outline because you already know the story itself, as reading it in this shortened form, focusing on what happens and leaving out much of the descriptive material will give you a good idea of how to write your own story outline. You pick on the most important points to focus on for a proposed script, rather than tell it as a detailed story in itself.

It should go something like this:

Rumpelstiltskin
One-page outline

A man who works as a miller is boasting about his daughter in a tavern. He tells all the people there that she can spin straw into gold. A servant from the palace hears the boast and hurries away to tell the King about it.

The King orders the girl to be brought to the palace. He tells her that she must spin some straw into gold for him or her father will be executed, but he also tells her that if she can do it he will marry her and she'll become Queen.

The girl is led to a small room filled with straw. She sits crying in despair. A strange little man appears and says that he can spin straw into gold and will gladly do it for her for a suitable payment.

She offers him a beautiful necklace and he does as promised and then disappears. The next day the King is delighted but not yet satisfied. He has the girl taken to a larger room filled with straw and tells her to get on with it. The same thing happens again: the strange little man appears, asks for payment, receives a gold ring from the girl's finger, sits down at the spinning wheel and gets stuck in.

The next day the King is pleased but reveals that he has one more room filled with straw that needs turning into gold before he will finally keep his promise.

So that night the girl is left alone in the room filled with straw and immediately the strange little man appears with his usual offer to help, but this time there's a snag. The girl has nothing left to give in payment. (Well, it *is* a story for children!) The little man, knowing of the King's promise to marry the girl, says he will work his magic just one more time if the girl will promise to give him her first-born child. She doesn't have much choice so she agrees.

The straw is spun. The King marries the girl. Everyone is about to live happily ever after until the Queen gives birth to a boy and the strange little man reappears to demand his payment.

The Queen is so distraught that the little man agrees to give her a chance to avoid handing over her child. He tells her that if she can guess his name he will call it quits. She is delighted but only has three days in which to do it. She writes down every single name she can think of and goes through the list with the strange little man on the first of his three visits. She draws a blank. The same thing happens on the second attempt and by now the Queen has sent her servants all over the surrounding countryside to gather unusual names.

Just before the strange little man arrives one of the servants comes into the Queen's room to give her some good news. Whilst walking in the woods this servant chanced upon the strange little man dancing around a fire and singing a song about what was happening. He sang of the Queen trying to guess his name and getting nowhere, and the lyrics included the name Rumpelstiltskin.

So now the Queen knows the man's name, but instead of just stating it she can't resist taunting him by pretending to get it wrong. Eventually, when she does say it to the strange little man, he gets really

> angry and stamps his foot so hard on the floor that he makes a hole in it and traps his foot. Then, still in a rage, he grabs hold of his own leg and pulls on it so hard that he tears himself in half.

End of strange little man and end of story, except for the rather unlikely one-line resolution that they all lived happily ever after – all except the strange little man, perhaps. (As suggested, this one-page outline is just under 700 words long.)

Now, ignoring the fact that there are some pretty big flaws in this story, such as why anyone would want to marry a King who's so cruel and greedy in the first place, or why a little man who can spin straw into gold couldn't just buy all the necklaces and rings he wanted, or why the girl should be cruel to the strange little man after he's saved her life and that of her father. Not to mention the structural weaknesses, like the story not starting with the main character and the main character not really solving her own problems but just getting lucky: first by meeting the strange little man without any effort and then by having a servant who just *happened* to stumble on the name Rumpelstiltskin at the very last minute.

Ignoring all this, there is still something pretty nasty about the whole thing. The strange little man didn't deserve to die. He wasn't wicked, just sad. So when I wrote the panto, instead of the strange little man killing himself in such a gruesome manner I had him burst into tears and say how lonely he had always been living in the forest all by himself, shunned by all and sundry. Then the Queen (who *didn't* taunt the strange little man in my version) felt sorry for him and invited him to live in the palace and look after the baby prince – effectively becoming the very first crèche manager. Now that's what I call a happy ending and the audience agreed.

I hope you can see this as an example of how your one-page outline can be changed and improved at any stage in the proceedings, but of course I'm supposed to be telling you how to take the next step and turn your one-page outline into a basic step outline.

Looking at the one-page outline of *Rumpelstiltskin* and following my own advice, I decided the first scene would have to take place in the tavern where the boastful miller starts the ball rolling. That would suitably set the tone, genre, style and location (once upon a time in a faraway land) and introduce the main character even if we didn't actually see her straight away.

In the second scene we'd get the hook when the King hears about the miller's boast and sends for the girl. Then of course we'd get progressive complications when the girl can't come up with the goods.

So my basic step outline started like this:

Scene 1 The miller boasts about daughter in pub.

Scene 2 A servant of the King who's heard the boast reports it to the King.

Then, jumping ahead, I wrote:

Scene 12 The Queen gets the name right. Offers job to Rumpelstiltskin. Happy ending.

And then I went back and filled in the blanks like this:

Scene 3 The King sends guards to miller's house for girl.

Scene 4 The King tells girl what she must do.

Scene 5	The girl can't spin straw into gold. Strange little man appears.
Scene 6	The King orders girl to do more.
Scene 7	Little man appears again.
Scene 8	King orders one more effort from girl.
Scene 9	Little man to rescue again but makes stronger demands.
Scene 10	King pleased. Marries girl.
Scene 11	Girl has baby. Little man reappears and makes her an offer.

Now you can see how I got to Scene 12, which reads:

Scene 12	The Queen gets the name right. Offers job to Rumpelstiltskin. Happy ending.

But I still had at least three more scenes involving the guessing of the name to fit in. That was no problem– I just scribbled out what I'd originally written for Scene 12 and carried on:

Scene 12	Girl gets name wrong. Tries to collect more names herself.
Scene 13	Girl gets name wrong again. Sends out servants collecting names.
Scene 14	Servants can't find new names, except one who's heard strange little man singing in forest.

Scene 15 Girl gets name right. Offers sad man a job. Happy ending.

As you can clearly see, I could easily cut out some of these scenes by having a narrator fill in the gaps or increase the number of scenes by splitting some of them in two, or decide that some of them weren't separate scenes to begin with but just one group of characters interrupting another group and so on. But none of this matters a damn. All that matters is that I can start turning my one-page outline into a basic scene-by-scene breakdown and do it in a matter of *minutes* instead of days.

In fact, I usually take just a couple of evenings to write these panto scripts, knowing we can add and subtract during rehearsals anyway. But the procedure is very similar to what I go through when I'm writing a TV script – only the intensity and the timescale is different.

If I can write a half-hour script in two evenings you can certainly write your calling-card script in ten weeks.

In case you're wondering, I advise my students to start with a step outline containing ten to fifteen scenes at first, because it can seem daunting to go straight for an outline with twenty-five to thirty or more scenes. It gives you great confidence to see how it works in a much simpler way at first. But please bear in mind that you can start by doing any number of scenes you think appropriate for you. There are no hard and fast rules for this procedure. I just know from years of experience that the students who follow my advice most willingly are usually the ones who learn fastest and then go on to invent their own methods.

More About Character Biographies

You might think it silly to write out biographies for

characters in a fairy story, but that's what I do when writing my pantomimes and, in fact, it makes perfect sense. The more 'real' these characters become the more people will care about them.

I wasn't impressed by the main characters in this story at all (as it's usually told.) The King is cruel and greedy. The miller is boastful and stupid. The heroine is beautiful but a bit vacuous and she cries a lot instead of standing up for herself and simply telling the truth – that she *can't* spin straw into gold and is a bit surprised that a King might think she could! Then later on she herself is cruel to the strange little man, taunting him by pretending she doesn't know his name when she does. And she's quite content to live happily ever after once the strange little man has committed suicide (or killed himself accidentally – whichever the coroner's verdict eventually comes up with).

The miller's wife doesn't even get a mention. And the one person in the story who acts honourably throughout is the strange little man. It's true that he asks a high price for his final night's work, but he's perfectly upfront about it and doesn't try to cheat anybody.

So I actually *did* give some moments of thought to all this. I decided the King needed to be kinder and have a good reason for wanting three roomfuls of gold. His largely agrarian kingdom had become poor following a couple of harsh winters and dry summers, and his subjects were suffering. He cared about all this so he wasn't such a bad bloke after all.

I decided the miller needed to be decent and lighthearted but a bit of a drinker, and his wife patient, kindly and worried about her talented daughter's future in these difficult times. And the girl herself needed to be loyal and forgiving towards her father for the position he'd put her in. She had to care so much for her father and mother that she was afraid to tell the truth about his boasts and put the blame on him.

I also decided that the strange little man should be a much more likable person. He wasn't wicked, just lonely and sad. Being so unusual in appearance, he couldn't get himself a partner even though he'd always longed for a family of his own. His desire for a child then became touching rather than sinister. And even nowadays in these more enlightened times, being single and 'different' he might find it difficult to get accepted by an adoption agency. Therefore his only chance of happiness was in somehow 'buying' himself a child.

Just a few random speculations like this might be all you need for *your* character biographies. Certainly enough to get you started. There's no need to go into too much detail.

I know I've said most of this before but just as a reminder:

Start with a name, and we've already talked about how important they can be. Give an age. Then a brief description of personality. Social class. Job or education. Things the person likes. Things they hate. Where you would most likely bump into them. Their general state of health. Any really traumatic experiences they've had. And that's probably enough. Don't strain to think of more things just to make a bigger list. Once they come alive you'll find out more anyway – hopefully even a few things that surprise you.

Don't describe the person physically in any detail unless it's really important and you're going to use it dramatically. Usually a general description – attractive, ordinary looking or whatever – will do for the time being.

Having got my basic step outline and my very brief character biographies, I am then ready to move on to the next thing.

The Detailed Step Outline

Once you've satisfied yourself that you have the main scenes sorted out in your basic step outline – that you have a beginning, middle and end for your main story and know a bit more about your characters – then you move on, straight away, to a longer and more detailed version, your detailed step outline.

You can either look at your basic outline as a whole and add more scenes to begin with *before* going through it one scene at a time adding details, or you can simply start at the beginning and focus on each scene but now writing a paragraph or two for each step instead of a single line or two. (Some scenes may be half a page or more – but still in prose, not in script form with dialogue.) Now you can pay more attention to the details of what's happening and also consider which character or characters offer the best chance for a sub-plot or two.

I usually prefer to start by focusing on Scene I at this stage and then work through each scene chronologically, adding details, rather than sketching the whole thing out as before. By now the characters are coming alive and don't seem so willing to be shuffled around like inanimate chess pieces.

Let me carry on using the Rumpelstiltskin outline as an example. The minute I looked again at the opening couple of lines in my basic step outline I realised I had a slight problem.

Why would a man suddenly tell everyone in a tavern that his daughter could spin straw into gold? It's not the kind of thing you casually slip into the conversation. (Well, not in any of the taverns that I find myself in.) On the other hand, he *was* in a tavern so he could have been drunk. That's a start, but even so it's unlikely he would have suddenly told such an outrageous lie out of the blue. Something must have prompted him into this exaggeration.

That's when I decided he'd be goaded into it by someone else who was boasting about *his* daughter and the boasts would escalate. It worked quite well and was funny. We had the tavern-keeper serving food to the miller, who said how nice it was. Then the tavern-keeper said what a wonderful cook his daughter was – and the miller said so was *his* daughter. Then the tavern-keeper said what a beautiful girl his daughter was and the miller responded in kind, but adding a bit more emphasis, and so on with each man becoming more competitive – going through housework, sense of humour, intelligence, kindness and dressmaking until there was nowhere else for the miller to go but spinning straw into gold!

That final blurted-out boast stunned everyone into silence, and of course the servant from the palace had already been given more information as well. The girl being talked about was not only a great cook – she was hard working, beautiful, kind hearted, talented and clever. A combination of Cindy Crawford, Delia Smith, Mother Teresa and Madame Curie all rolled into one. On top of all that, she could spin straw into gold. No wonder the person who worked at the palace thought the King might be interested.

So, having planned out the first scene in some detail (still not using dialogue, just the gist of what's being said), the second scene in the palace was easy to plan. We'd see the King moaning to someone about how his subjects longed for a Queen who would give them an heir to the throne, but that he was so concerned about saving them all from poverty that he couldn't even think of getting married. (And of course this had the effect of making the King seem much nicer than he is in the original story.)

Then, in thinking about the third scene, I wondered what might have happened to the miller once he got home, sobered up a bit and remembered what he'd been saying in the tavern. Might he feel embarrassed and try to explain, just in case somebody else mentioned it first? We got another funny scene out of this, with him saying how he'd been telling everyone what a wonderful daughter he had, and his wife and daughter both being pleased until he casually mentioned the bit about spinning straw into gold. Then they were concerned, saying how serious it could be if someone important heard about this, but they concluded that nobody would have taken it seriously. And of course that's when there was a loud knock at the door.

Having already planned out each scene in skeleton form it was fun to go through it adding details in this way (in longhand and in my notepad). Some of the characters had developed into more fully-rounded personalities, so by the time I wrote the dialogue I felt as if I knew them. I didn't *have* to make up the dialogue – the characters spoke for themselves. And that's exactly what can happen with your script if you tackle it in this way.

I know there will be more pressure on you to write a TV script that might one day make your work accessible to millions of people than there ever could be to write a panto for your local church, but in essence it's the same. You want to do the best job you can. One of my TV episodes drew an audience of eight and a half million viewers. My biggest audience for a church panto was closer to one hundred and fifty. Obviously I cared about them both, but the pressure is different. Writing something for your friends is like playing football for your local pub team, but writing for TV is more like playing for Manchester United or Arsenal.

That's why I'm advising you to spend ten weeks writing your script, not two evenings. But don't let yourself become overawed. Those one hundred and fifty people sitting in the church hall are no different from the people sitting at home watching TV. In fact they are the same people, there are just fewer of them.

9 Fine Tuning

One-minute Overview

In this chapter you'll learn some more about using dialogue effectively. You'll then be reassured about what an experienced script-reader means when he or she talks about 'character development'. You'll be shown how to turn problems into opportunities. You'll be told how to eliminate coincidence, making your script even stronger in the process, and you'll be given a few examples of how a 'good' scene can be turned into a possibly 'great' one.

Dialogue That Ruins a Script

I've already talked in great detail about dialogue, so is there anything left to say? Well, yes, because dialogue is probably fifty per cent of a TV drama and as such demands a lot of thought and care.

I want to return to something I said much earlier about on-the-nose dialogue – that is dialogue that tells us things in too obvious a way. Remember the examples I gave, of a person doing something and telling us about it at the same time? Handing someone a cup of tea and saying, 'Tea, wasn't it?' And about one character telling another character all about something that we, the audience, had already seen?

That's bad enough, but at least it's believable and natural. In real life people do say things they don't need to say, or tell each other in detail about encounters they've just had. No, there's something even worse. It's when people get together and start telling each other things that *they* would already know, or that they probably wouldn't say in such precise detail. Then it becomes immediately obvious that they are not really talking to each other but just giving information to the audience. I'm sure you know the kind of thing I mean.

Two people bump into each other in the street and the conversation goes something like this.

Bill: John. Fancy meeting you here on a Wednesday afternoon on a street in the middle of a mainly industrial city in the heart of the Midlands. Just as I'm on my way to the hospital to get the results of my recent heart and lung scan.

John: Bill. What a pleasant surprise and only a few yards from the primary school we both attended as lads until we left in 1952 at the age of eleven. You to go on to grammar school and me to the local comprehensive. But what's this about a heart scan? You used to be a real athlete and signed amateur forms for Derby County before breaking both ankles rescuing a pit pony from a quarry.

John: Aye, but them days are long gone and as you know I spent thirty years working for your father in his asbestos factory after that. And all that time married to Joan – the girl you always fancied and never stopped wanting – even after she had the son my doctor thought she'd never have because I was supposed to be infertile ...

And so on. Yes, I've exaggerated a little bit but I have heard dialogue *nearly* as crass and obvious as this. I'm always puzzled when it actually gets onto the screen. I can't believe that script-editors, producers and directors have all let it pass. You only have to glance at it to see that it's not only unbelievable but also written in those undesirable chunks and that too 'correct' style I told you to watch out for. I'm surprised that the actors can do it with a straight face, but it still happens. Maybe it's something to do with things being done in a rush and there being no time to do it again. Obviously there will be times like this in any job, but the important thing for you to remember is: don't do it!

Make a note

- Read again the five functions of dialogue (see p. 52).
- Then cut any dialogue you don't need.

Character Development

Sometimes a script-editor will say that the characters haven't developed throughout your script. This can be a frightening comment if taken too literally. Are you *really* expected to create characters that change slowly from moment to moment as people do in real life, maturing and constantly modifying their opinions? Growing like flowers grow from bulbs until they finally reach full blossom?

The good news is that you are not expected to do this, especially not in a piece lasting just thirty minutes. What you *are* expected to do is make sure at least one of your characters has changed in some way from what they were like at the beginning of your script into what they've become at the end. That's what drama is all about – people changing because of the things that happen to them (or that they make happen).

They don't necessarily change slowly and gradually. They might change in an instant after experiencing something that has a profound effect upon them. Your main character might change substantially, from a miserable old miser like Ebenezer Scrooge at the beginning of Dickens's great classic to a generous and happy-go-lucky benefactor at the end of it. Even here, however, the change wasn't all that gradual a process. Scrooge stayed miserly for quite a while, and as for the other characters it's hard to remember any of them changing very much at all. So if a genius like Dickens didn't have to do it organically throughout a whole book, it's obvious that you won't be expected to do it in a thirty-minute piece.

Just make sure that *something* has happened that leaves your main character, at least, a changed person: happier, sadder, more downcast, triumphant or whatever.

Make a note	• Character development basically just means that a change has taken place.

Meeting Problems Head On

As a writer you should welcome problems in your script because that's what drama is all about – people trying to solve problems. Without a problem to solve the main character in your script wouldn't be involved in a drama or comedy in the first place. And if the problem to be solved is too simple it won't prove much of a challenge for characters and audience alike. So it follows that the more experience you have as a problem solver yourself, the better you'll become at creating problems and using them to your advantage through the characters.

I read somewhere about lions out hunting in a pack. Apparently the older and bigger lions will sometimes deliberately show themselves to their prey and then give a loud roar. This terrifies the animals being hunted so they turn and run in the opposite direction – straight into the path of the younger and faster lions lying in wait. If the animals being hunted only knew it they would stand much more chance of getting away if they ran directly towards the lions making all the noise. It also wouldn't do an antelope much good to simply stand still and hope the lions would mistake it for a garden ornament. So in general it's better to 'run towards the roar'.

Whenever you have a tricky problem with your script or your characters, don't run away or decide to do nothing in the hope that nobody will notice – welcome the problem and meet it head on. By solving it you will invariably make your script (and yourself) stronger. There is *always* an answer and, if you decide there isn't, you shouldn't have got your characters into that situation in the first place. You need to go further back in your script and make some changes.

Very occasionally an exasperated student will say to me, 'But it isn't *real* you know. It's just a story I'm making up.' The implication being: who cares why he or she is doing whatever they're doing? Then I know that particular student is likely to struggle. If your story and your characters don't come alive for you, how will they ever do that for an audience?

The funny thing is that fiction often needs to be *more* 'real' than real life – not less. We all know that incredible things sometimes happen in real life. People get lucky breaks they seem to have done nothing to deserve and so on. But good drama isn't about random happenings, it's about things done wilfully by the characters in your story. Without that 'cause and effect' progression they don't really register. They're not important.

It would be a bit like taking a dart and throwing it at a dartboard, without taking aim, and finding you'd hit the double top. You might be surprised or even impressed but it wouldn't be *significant* – not unless you were actually aiming for it in order to win a prize and you'd never thrown a dart in your life. Then it wouldn't be credible unless it was supposed to be funny.

In a badly written sitcom you sometimes get a character who is supposed to be stupid suddenly doing something really clever or delivering a really telling line. The writer has been unable to resist doing this to push the story along, or just to use the telling line he or she (not the character) has thought of. Similarly, you'll see the opposite happening too. A character who is supposed to be really clever will fail to spot something that's blindingly obvious to everyone else. Again, this is lazy writing. You should avoid it.

In fact, you can usually make things like this work for you. You can have a stupid character doing or saying something really clever and explain it later by having a reason for it. Suppose, for instance, the stupid character makes some profound statement on world affairs and everyone is surprised and delighted until they realise he or she has just heard it on a children's quiz show? And a clever person could *seem* to be acting stupidly but have a secret reason for doing so – they might be trying to boost someone else's confidence, for instance. But just to allow your characters (*force* them, actually) to do something completely out of character merely weakens them and your drama as a whole.

Go back to what I said about learning from your problems. I remember an incident that happened very early in my career as a teacher in a junior school. I had written the annual Christmas pantomime and was holding auditions. Two little girls desperately wanted to be the Fairy Godmother and it was quite difficult to choose between them. The little girl not chosen instantly burst into tears and said she'd *never* had a good part in the Christmas play and this was her last chance because she'd be leaving the school next summer. I felt very sorry for her but couldn't change my mind and disappoint the other little girl.

I didn't know what to do for a moment and then one of the other children made the simplest of suggestions. 'I know, sir,' she said, 'Why not have *two* Fairy Godmothers?' This was a moment of revelation for me because, as obvious as the suggestion was, it was something I'd never really thought about – changing the script to suit the occasion.

Like most people, I automatically assumed that once you had the script that was it: you simply found people to fit the parts and got on with it.

It had never occurred to me that it was *my* script and I could do anything I wanted with it. I was behaving as if there were unbreakable rules, which was crazy. I quickly rewrote part of the script to include a trainee Fairy Godmother. And the two characters bickering, with the trainee Fairy Godmother being overenthusiastic and getting spells wrong, and the *real* Fairy Godmother getting flustered as she tried to put things right, became one of the best things in the show.

It taught me a lesson I've never forgotten. Problems should be used as stepping-stones – not something to be avoided at all costs.

Make a note

- Don't underestimate your audience.
- Don't misuse your characters.
- Don't think people won't notice if you try to cheat them.
- Solving problems is what drama is all about – so don't avoid them.
- Run towards the roar.

Getting Rid of Coincidence

Coincidences can often seem incredible and, just like problems, they happen to all of us in one form or another. But again, they usually happen at random so don't always make for good drama. One coincidence near the beginning of a thirty-minute drama, to set things moving, can be fine but any more than that, especially if used to solve a problem, smacks of lazy writing.

It can be different with a comedy. An incident from an old *Batman* episode has stuck in my mind for over forty years Batman and Robin are in a helicopter that's about to crash on the outskirts of a large city. Looking down at all the buildings and the traffic far below, Robin is a bit concerned. Then Batman calmly tells him not to worry because he's remembered something, they just happen to be flying above an area where there's a 'used mattress disposal facility' (or some such expression – I can't remember the exact words). And sure enough, there below them is a huge pile of mattresses just waiting to be disposed of, like a purpose-built helipad only to be used in emergencies. This made me laugh out loud – at the absurdity of the idea itself and at the very unlikely coincidence – and I was an adult watching a show primarily aimed at children.

As it happens, I am a great collector of coincidences myself. I was, for instance, once sitting in an office at the BBC talking to a script-editor when the phone rang. On the phone was one of my brothers calling from his house in Derby. Naturally, once he had given his name and said where he was calling from, the script-editor assumed the call was for me. But it wasn't. My brother had no idea I was in London that day or even that I was currently writing something for the BBC. It was nothing more than a coincidence.

He had met a lady in Brighton some days earlier and they'd swapped phone numbers. The number she had given him was for an agency in London hiring out office temps. My brother had called the agency and been given a number to call. He didn't realise at the time that this number was for an office at the BBC studios where the woman was currently being employed. And she just happened to be working for my script-editor. The script-editor couldn't quite believe it for a moment and thought that my brother was joking when he explained what had happened.

We all thought the coincidence was weird. Just imagine how many people might have been shopping in Brighton on the day that my brother was there, and how many offices there must be in London – not to mention how many there are in the BBC studio itself – you will realise what kind of odds we are talking about here.

On another occasion I was on holiday in Florida and started talking to a very nice man from Slough. I had only ever really known one other person from Slough in my life – over twenty years before when we were both doing National Service together in Singapore. He was a man I'd liked very much at the time but, as with most army friends, never thought of keeping in touch with him – so in a rather weak attempt at a humorous introduction I said to the man in Florida, 'Ah. Slough. So you'd know Michael Binnington then?'

The man gave me a very surprised look and said, 'Yes I do. He's my best friend.' I assumed he was joking, but he wasn't. He assumed I was being serious but I wasn't. He thought that his wife must have mentioned Michael to me in an earlier conversation, but we hadn't even said hello before that moment. It was just another coincidence. I found out afterwards that Slough has a population of over one hundred thousand people. I'd only ever met two of them, quite separately, with a gap of thirty years between the two meetings, and they just happened to be best friends.

I could go on and on because coincidences, insignificant or sometimes surprisingly apt, seem to happen to me a lot. But I would never consider using one to solve a problem in a script. Coincidences are amusing in real life but can be irritating and unconvincing in a drama, and they are rarely necessary. If you find a way to avoid coincidence you will almost invariably make your script stronger.

Instead of things just happening for no apparent reason it's better if someone takes action to *make* them happen. This gives credit to one of your characters for having the initiative to try something and also gives credit to you as the writer.

So, suppose a married woman out with her friends just happens to spot her husband in a bar with another woman. If that occurs at the beginning of a drama it will be accepted and possibly even enjoyed, but if it comes at a point where the woman actually *needs* to see her husband because she's in danger it would be unsatisfying. Much better if the woman has to struggle to get in touch with him and finally achieves it.

Make a note

- Only use coincidence near the beginning of a drama.
- Never use more than one coincidence in a thirty-minute drama.
- Avoid using coincidence to solve problems.
- Coincidences can be very effective in a comedy but, again, not too many.

Producing 'Magic Moments'

The artistic director I mentioned earlier from the Derby Playhouse, David Milne, also introduced me to the idea of having 'magic moments' in your script. David was talking about the stage, but the concept works equally well for TV and film.

Magic moments are those bits of a show that people remember for years and talk about whenever the show is discussed. I've already mentioned one – The scene in *Stepping Out* when the sunlight comes through the stained-glass window and becomes a spotlight and Liza Minnelli dances. There are several more magic moments in this film, the finale itself, where the amateur tap dancers achieve a glorious (and entirely believable) triumph, being just one of them.

Most sitcom lovers will remember the scene where David Jason, as Del Boy Trotter (*Only Fools and Horses*, BBC TV), leans back to rest his elbow on a bar flap that isn't there and disappears from sight – exactly at the moment when he's trying to impress a couple of women. Then there's the roller-skating sequence from *Some Mothers Do 'Ave 'Em* that just builds and builds until the chaotic ending that gets a spontaneous round of applause from the studio audience (and maybe from the people watching it at home on television).

Another one that sticks out in my mind is the final shoot out from *Shane.* The tension that's been building throughout most of the film gathers intensity as Alan Ladd, the hero, rides into town to confront Jack Pallance, as the villain (and perhaps sundry others too who may be lurking in the shadows of the saloon). Scenes intercut from the hero riding resolutely onwards – to the interior of the dimly-lit saloon bar – and then to a young boy who is following the hero. We have a pretty good idea what's going to happen (especially, as in my case, after seeing it for the twenty-fifth time!) but it's still powerful and gripping.

I could go on citing similar sequences for hours, and I'm sure that most of you could do the same. But is it possible to learn something from this? How do you go about creating a magic moment or two for your own script?

Well, for a start it's obvious that the writers and directors of the shows mentioned put a lot of thought into what they did. But they do that all the time. They want every scene to be as good as it can possibly be. So what did they do to make certain moments more special than others? I'd say they would actually select a certain scene that they know is 'good' and focus on it with the deliberate intention of making it stand out. It's yet another way of adding variety. If you did this with too many scenes the film or TV show as a whole would lose pace. You simply can't allow the audience to stop and focus intently on scene after scene, so you do it with just a few.

One way to heighten a scene like this is by turning someone on the screen (or a number of people on the screen) into spectators themselves. They are suddenly watching the action as much as we are, but from a closer angle. This somehow gives an extra poignancy to what the 'actual' viewer is watching. We know what *we* are feeling but that's enhanced by us also knowing what the 'audience' on screen is feeling. If what happens makes both them and us happy then our feelings are magnified by what seems like a shared experience.

This trick is used very successfully in three of the examples given above. When Liza Minnelli dances so sublimely after the sunlight hits her, we cut away to see that she's being observed by one of her female pupils who's entered the room without being seen. We can read this admiring student's thoughts as she watches in awe. Then, in the final sequence, there's a whole theatre filled with rapturous spectators all applauding wildly.

Similarly, when Del Boy falls backwards so spectacularly in the bar we know that the girls he's been trying to impress will be in fits of laughter and that will make him feel even worse. We sympathise with him to a certain extent but can't help finding it hilarious, just as the watching girls would.

And when Alan Ladd reaches the saloon, the young boy who's following him arrives just in time to see it all from his spot on the floor beneath the batwing doors. From time to time we flash away from the main protagonists to see what effect the growing tension, and then the action, is having on the boy. In a sense it's almost identical to the way the scene with the dance sequence was handled and in both cases our feelings are enhanced.

Why not try to add just a couple of 'magic moments' to your script?

Make a note

- Magic moments are created when good scenes are made even better.
- You can add to the viewer's emotion by having an 'audience' on screen.

10 Into the Home Stretch

One-minute Overview

In this chapter you will really get to grips with the writing of your first 'professional' script. You'll be taken from first draft to the polished item, ready to be sent out in a 'correct' TV layout. You'll be told how to use friends to help you achieve a thoroughly workable script. You'll be reminded of structure and given some examples of what's needed for a satisfying ending. You'll be provided with checklists so you can be confident that nothing's been left out and you've done the best job you're capable of doing.

First Draft and 'Improvised Dialogue'

It should be an exciting moment when you've got your very first *detailed* step outline in front of you. Let me reassure you, when you've reached this point you've probably done the hardest part. All you have to do now is let the characters you've created come alive and take over. If you've done a good job so far they should be bursting to do that.

So let them get on with it. Just start adding dialogue and 'directions' to your outline, but work fast and go straight through your script from start to finish without going back to do rewrites. That doesn't mean you have to try to do it in one session, though you might find yourself doing that. It just means you don't write one scene, then stop and go back to rewrite it. You write one scene and move straight on to the next scene, like a sprinter with the finishing line in sight from the moment you hear the starting pistol. Don't worry about trying to get the dialogue and visuals just 'right'. That would be like the same sprinter stopping halfway down the course to comb her hair and straighten her vest in anticipation of the cameras waiting near the winner's podium.

At this point in time your goal is just to get from the beginning of your outline to the end as quickly as possible. Any hesitation here can be costly and ineffective. Just keep going, using straightforward 'improvised' dialogue. Let the characters say the first words that come to mind to push your story along in the right direction, and let them take whatever action seems appropriate at the time. Don't worry about making mistakes, it's so much easier to change things once you've done it all.

I've always seen this process as a sort of journey through a thick jungle to reach a mountaintop. You have a compass bearing (your outline), so you know you're on the right track but you can't avoid stepping into the odd swamp or having to swim across a river or two. You don't keep doubling back in the hope of finding a better way – you just plod on, knowing that it's only when you get to the top of the mountain and look back that you can see an easier route, an easier route you could so easily have missed by turning back earlier, whilst you were still lost in the trees.

Bearing that in mind, take a deep breath and get stuck in. Don't look back until you've finished. When you've done that don't show your script to anyone. Unless you are all fired up to do some *obvious* rewrites, I'd advise you to put your script to one side and take a day or two off. Go for walks in the park, go off on a day trip, treat somebody special to a nice meal or generally do *anything* you fancy that has nothing to do with any form of writing you can think of. Whatever you do, don't start doing *detailed* rewrites involving dialogue straight away.

Edit and Rewrite

Now you're ready to look through your script and see where the weaknesses are in terms of structure and storyline. You can still ignore the dialogue at this point. And please note: don't worry about 'correct' script layout until you're ready to do the copies you are going to submit. Don't waste paper by leaving large margins or by beginning each scene on a new page. Use any format that suits you until *after* the read-through session I'll be describing very soon.

For now – ask yourself these questions:

- Have I set the location, genre and tone straight away?
- Are the main characters introduced quickly and effectively?
- Is there a good 'hook' in the first minute or two?
- Have I made it perfectly clear whose story this is?
- Is there any loss of focus on pivotal character/s?
- Are the stakes raised high enough?
- Have I dealt with any sub-plots clearly enough?
- Are there any loose ends that need tying up?
- Has at least one character other than the main character worked out their 'agenda'?
- Is there one scene I could turn into a real 'magic moment'?
- Is the climax exciting enough?
- Is the resolution short, sharp and effective?

And please also note:

1. I am still advising you *not* to rewrite the dialogue at this point (even with regard to any 'magic moments').

2. You may have realised that, although you've already practised some of the things mentioned in the above list, you *haven't* been encouraged to have a practice go at writing a climax. The reasons for this will probably be obvious. Although you can easily make up a duologue, an opening sequence and even a larger cast sequence, it's not quite the same thing to conjure up something that comes near the end of a show. The success or otherwise of any climax is inextricably linked to what's gone before it and how

well you reincorporate aspects of this into it. So without going through the whole process of planning a script and writing quite a lot of it first, this would be like trying to put icing on a cake before it goes into the oven.

Climax and Resolution

Perhaps the one thing we *can* do at this point is have a look at a few examples from other people's work and see what can be learned from them. It would certainly be a good exercise for you to study the endings of some of your own favourite films and TV dramas. Try to work out what it is that makes some endings more exciting and satisfying than others. Here are a few things to consider:

- Is there enough at stake?
- Is the challenge to the main character big enough?
- Does the main character play the most decisive part?
- Is there some kind of last-gasp hiccup that supplies a final twist?
- Is the final resolution suitably short and satisfying?

As a child I was mad about action movies. Sometimes the makers of these films went to ridiculous lengths to encompass the factors listed above. The stakes were certainly high enough – sometimes people battling for whole countries – but still the need to personalise the thing (and highlight the main character) took precedence.

In the midst of a massive battle the main character on the 'good' army's side would somehow be the only person on the battlefield to notice the main villain on the 'bad' army's side sneaking away, leaving his faithful but misguided followers to perish whilst he made his escape. The hero would leap onto a horse and chase the villain, usually around a group of boulders in California, even if they were supposed to be Saxons fighting against Normans on the south coast of England (because Hollywood was where 'big' films were made) and there'd be a fist-fight which the hero narrowly won.

Then came the hiccup. Just as the hero turned his back on his beaten opponent (to acknowledge the arrival of his best friend and the female love-interest, who'd both followed him in case he needed help), the villain would pull a knife from his waistband and try to plunge it into the hero's back. The hero's love-interest would shout a timely warning and the hero's best friend would throw his own knife towards the hero, who would catch it and kill the villain. The best friend would tell the hero that the battle was won. The hero would embrace the woman and say something about one day seeing a schoolroom built on that very spot. End of story.

It made me wonder why no one ever made a film about the Second World War that ended with Hitler jumping on a horse and galloping madly across the desert with Winston Churchill, Field Marshal Montgomery and Dame Vera Lynn all in hot pursuit. (I hope that's not spoilt an idea you've been working on yourself!)

Films and TV dramas aren't quite *that* naïve these days but the conventions still apply to some extent. There is still the build up of tension and the need for the main character to be instrumental in deciding the outcome. It doesn't matter how many police officers are involved, or even a crack SAS unit, the villain will still be thwarted by the drama's main character, even if that person happens to be a twelve-year-old girl with only her school satchel as a weapon. And there will usually still be a hiccup, when the stakes are suddenly raised, followed by the triumph and the pay off. It *still* works. Handled properly it's what people want to see.

In a *Rocky*-type film we know very well that the hero is going to end up as a world champion boxer, and that's what we want. But we don't want it to be too easy for him.

We don't want to see the hero climb into the ring and knock his opponent out with one punch, nor do we want to see him grind out a narrow points victory with people arguing over the ref's decision (either of which could happen in real life).

No. When our hero climbs into the ring for the final battle we need to feel he's the underdog with only the slightest chance of success. He might make a good start but we know that at some point he's going to take a battering, and that at least some of the people in his corner are going to plead with him to give up before he gets killed. That's the hiccup bit. That's when the hero summons up one last ounce of strength and courage, possibly after seeing his wife mouthing the words, 'You can do it' in the crowd, and goes out and flattens his opponent with a superhuman barrage of punches. And that's when the wife, perhaps estranged at this point and not even supposed to be in the same city, climbs into the ring to say she still loves him after all. That's what drama is all about. Meeting high expectations.

Now you should be ready to start again at the beginning of your script and rewrite the whole thing, including the dialogue (and *still* not in 'correct' script layout unless that's what you'd prefer). Before you do anything else, however, stop for a while to make sure you remember all I've been saying about dialogue throughout the book. In case you don't remember, let me say what the three biggest dangers are at this point:

1. You will write too much dialogue. You must remember that 'this is show business – not tell business' and cut every word you don't really need. If the audience can understand something without it being said, don't say it. Let the actors and the visuals do it for you. Don't have one character telling us that another character is a nasty piece of work. Let us see it for ourselves with the character *being* nasty.

2. Your dialogue will all sound the same no matter who is speaking. Because you are writing the dialogue you are lending your own voice to every character. If you happen to be well educated and witty perhaps you're making all your characters sound like this too, even if they are supposed to be uneducated and deeply serious. Don't do this. Let each of them speak with their own voice.
3. Your dialogue will be too literary and 'correct'. Look at your dialogue on the page. Do you see regular 'clumps' of dialogue with sentences that are neat and tidy? Or do you have a mixture of smaller and longer sentences that are sometimes unfinished and sometimes just single words? The first example isn't natural – the second is. Don't have characters making little speeches to each other. Have them interrupting sometimes, and also saying their sentences in the slightly jumbled way that most people do in real life.

Next time you're at a get-together of any kind (a wedding perhaps, or a business meeting) notice how differently a speaker sounds when he or she is reading from a prepared text or simply improvising from sketchy notes. Much depends on the quality of the speaker, of course, but in general which do you find is usually the most pleasant to listen to? Can you imagine listening to a stand-up comedian reading jokes from a script? It's rather strange to think that we use a virtually different language when we're writing compared with when we are speaking.

Unless you are feeling *really* confident don't just rely on these three points. Go back and read the five rules again and be prepared to trim, trim, trim those excess words.

Once you've rewritten the whole script from start to finish, you will have your very first completed draft copy (but still not necessarily in 'correct' script layout). Don't worry if some parts of it feel more like the seventh or eight draft. Remember, it's only the *final* draft that really matters. Perhaps we should call this the first completed draft that's good enough to be shown to other people (meaning your friends – not professionals). There will still be changes to make, but all the really hard work has been done, and you are back to the 'fun' part. Run off two or three extra copies, buy a bottle of wine (or two), make a few sandwiches and invite some friends round.

Act Out and Polish

If you want to be really professional about this it's a good idea to let your friends read the script to themselves *before* you get them together to act it out. This is what would happen in a real situation. The actors cast in the various parts would have a copy of the rehearsal script sent to their homes, and wouldn't be expected to read it out loud on first sight.

Let me remind you that the script you write will be called the 'rehearsal' script until it's re-typed after the director's comments have been included. Then it will become the 'shooting' script. But let's keep this as simple as possible. You may not want to go to the trouble of casting your friends in various parts and then talking to them individually about any queries they may have. This is time consuming and not always easy to arrange. If you *can* do it, of course, it might be a great help (though you should consider limiting each person to asking questions about their own character, so you don't run the risk of getting confused by more general comments at this stage).

So, moving on ... you've got a bunch of friends round and you've given out enough copies of the script so they can read it without too much hesitation. If possible allocate parts as suitably as you can, otherwise just do your best.

Some people may have to play several parts, and if they end up having a conversation with themselves it can cause unintended laughter and confusion. Obviously you should try to avoid this, but on balance *any* kind of acted-out effort is better than none at all, even if it comes down to two people reading alternate lines. You will still get to *hear* your dialogue, rather than just keep reading it silently, and you should benefit enormously from this. On no account should you ever send out a script that you haven't heard read aloud. As I've said before, we simply don't write dialogue as naturally as we speak it and even the most experienced scriptwriters tend to write passages of dialogue that look all right on the page but turn out to be over wordy, if not 'unsayable', in the rehearsal room. Sort this out as much as you can *before* your script is read by an expert.

So what I'm advising you to do for this exercise is: cast your drama as well as you can amongst your friends and acquaintances, and don't include yourself. You can read out the directions and scene headings yourself if you feel the need to keep a measure of control over the proceedings, but if you feel confident enough ask someone else to do this while you sit quietly with your notepad and pencil at the ready.

Request everyone *not* to ask questions once the read-through has started and explain that you are going to time it. (This is true, but it's also a good excuse to keep them focused on just getting through the script without arguing with each other.) And please note: your timing doesn't have to be deadly accurate. Three or four minutes either way won't be noticed.

Before starting, you can tell them that you'll welcome questions *afterwards* and that these questions can be either specific to their character or more general in nature: to do with storyline, structure or theme (or anything at all that they didn't understand or weren't sure about). After all, if these people who have studied the script to a certain extent have difficulties with it, it's likely that *anyone* reading it for the first time will feel exactly the same.

You then sit and listen and make notes. You will probably find you've written too much dialogue in your script and can cut lots of words and even whole sentences without losing anything. Remember what was said earlier in this book: 'If something doesn't need to be said – don't say it.'

You may also realise that certain characters have got lost in some scenes (and a friend who's gone a page or two without saying a line or getting involved will be very eager indeed to tell you about it). Or you may find that the main storyline becomes blurred. There may also be loose ends to sub-plots. Maybe the climax isn't exciting enough and needs more of a build up? Maybe there is an opportunity to raise the stakes somewhere or produce a 'magic moment'?

When the read-through is finished thank everyone and ask for comments. If you've noticed anyone struggling with their lines ask about that too. Whatever you do, *don't* get into an argument. These people have done you a big favour. That doesn't mean you can't defend your ideas – just do it quietly and sensibly.

One thing I always tell my students in any group discussion is to listen to suggestions (and criticisms) patiently and with consideration. Never dismiss anything straight away, however unreasonable and unhelpful it might appear to be. On the other hand it does no harm to mention the fact that you'd prefer *constructive advice* rather than *destructive comments.* Tell them you are looking for ways to improve your script, not ways to pull it to pieces. That's usually a good way to get them to focus on being positive rather than negative and it's not necessarily an easy option.

If they can't come up with ideas to help, you should know instinctively if that's because the script is so good it doesn't need help or that it's so bad it can't be rescued. Just don't risk getting into an argument that spirals downwards. As far as possible, try to look at your own script as if it's just an object that you like and are hoping others will like too. Don't look at it as if it's your only child that you've just given birth to. It might feel like that, but it really isn't.

Don't take any criticism personally. In some cases it's just a matter of taste. The fact that one of your friends doesn't like cheese-and-tomato sandwiches doesn't mean that you are stupid because you've just offered her one, nor will it mean that millions of other people are going to stop eating them either. Have the courage of your convictions. If you feel what you've written is good, then say so but say it politely, and be grateful that your friends are taking the exercise seriously. The worst thing they can do is simply lie to avoid hurting your feelings, and by doing that lull you into a false sense of security. You want their genuine opinions not their unstinting praise.

However, suppose you've had six friends doing your read-through and *all* of them make the same criticisms (or even a clear majority). That's the time to give what they're saying more consideration. They could still be wrong, but you might be wise to think again. On the other hand, if the criticisms are mixed and people start arguing over one point or another, you can assume that it's pretty safe to ignore what they're saying and continue making your own decisions.

Whatever happens, you should have learned a lot from this exercise.

Make a note

- Don't expect friends to do a good read-through at first sight.
- Don't take part yourself.
- Listen and take notes without interrupting.
- Ask your friends not to interrupt the read-through either.
- Time it – roughly.
- Don't take criticisms personally.
- If a majority of people make the same criticism – listen carefully.
- If opinions vary, go with your own gut reaction.

Print Out Your Polished Script in a 'Correct' TV Layout

Maybe you've already done this but, if not, turn to the appendix and follow the instructions given. If you have any difficulties at all in setting up the shortcut keys, just ask a friend to help. It's a lot simpler than it looks at first glance and the results are well worth the effort.

11 You Deserve Promotion

One-minute Overview

In this chapter we'll get back to the mechanics of the process. You'll be told where and how to submit your script copies. You'll be told something about the realities of approaching an agent at this stage in your development. You'll be reminded of how vitally important your attitude can be. You'll learn that 'selling' a script can demand almost as much creative energy as writing it in the first place. You'll be told how best to cope with rejection, how to welcome feedback and how to move on from there.

Where and How to Submit Your Calling-card Script

If we are talking here about using your script purely as an example of your work, then the answer regarding *where* to send it is fairly simple. You should already know which programmes you would like to write for, so just run off the relevant number of script copies and prepare to get on with it. Approach them all at the same time if that's what you want to do.

To find out exactly where to send your script, simply take a look at the credits that appear at the end of the particular show. They will tell you who made it and then, if necessary, you can check for the full contact details in a reference book like the *Writers' and Artists' Yearbook* or *The Writer's Handbook*. The BBC also has a website where you can find all sorts of information. I find it confusing to keep lists of 'correct' website addresses, but I usually get what I want by simply typing something like 'BBC Writers' Guidelines' or 'BBC Writersroom' into the search engine.

If you don't want to take any chances on your script

getting lost, you can always make your initial contact by phone. Just explain to whoever answers that you have a script you'd like to send to (name the programme) and then ask for the correct name and address. Be polite and friendly but also try to be confident. You are a writer looking for work, not a down-and-out begging for a handout. You might be doing *them* a favour. But it's as well not to expect anyone to be particularly welcoming or encouraging at first. Unsolicited scripts are never in short supply. As I said earlier, many of them aren't very good at all and the person you are speaking to has no way of knowing how brilliant yours might be.

Just remember what I said earlier, and be optimistic and gently persistent. If you happen to be put through to someone who doesn't just give you the information you want but asks you about yourself, don't panic. Respond in an honest (well, *basically* honest) and positive way. If they ask you what kind of things you've written before, don't put yourself down by saying, 'Oh nothing really.' Say something like, 'Oh lots of things, but not for TV until now.' Then hope they don't have time to ask for details, so you won't have to confess you've mostly written notes for the milkman or your children's schoolteachers.

I once gave an interview on my local radio station telling about how busy I'd been for the past year or so writing material for every top comedy performer in the country. I came away feeling pretty pleased with myself until the next day I got a call from a tax inspector who'd heard the broadcast and been suitably impressed. But now he wanted to know why I hadn't declared most of those earnings in my last statement. I had the embarrassing job of explaining to him that although I hadn't told any lies on the radio and I really *had* been writing for Ken Dodd, Les Dawson, the Two Ronnies and Morecambe and Wise, I just hadn't actually managed to sell very much of it. Luckily he had a sense of humour and wished me better luck in the future.

So exaggerating your own importance *can* backfire, but it's still a better policy than putting yourself down.

If you are talking to someone who says something like, 'Sorry but we only look at scripts sent through an agent,' then you mustn't just say, 'Okay, I won't bother then' and put the phone down. You're supposed to be a creative writer – so be creative. Say something like, 'Yes, I thought that might be the case but, as you know, it isn't easy for a new writer to get started. I'm quite pleased with this script and I was just hoping you might make an exception.' Whatever they say after that, try to make sure you *do* get the name and address you want.

Then think about sending the script anyway, despite what they've said about not reading scripts that don't come via an agent. You never know if it might get there on a particularly slack day, or if someone will open it and start reading *before* they notice the blank space where an agent's name and address is supposed to be. Or, if you think that might be a waste of time and money, consider sending them a letter to follow up on your phone call, or try to get an agent or do *something* positive. Whatever you do, don't hang around feeling sorry for yourself. Just move briskly on to the next show you want to try for. This is a very competitive business, and remember what I said about persistence being so important. Unless you are blessed with incredible luck nothing is going to be handed to you on a plate.

Send your scripts out all over the place and keep doing it. You might get lucky straight away and get the recognition you deserve. But if you keep your scripts at home in a drawer and wait for some hungry TV producer to come knocking, I promise you'll wait a very long time.

We've dealt with where to send your script and about how to prepare for this but now let's think about the actual mechanics of presentation. Print out your script in the manner shown in the appendix of this book. Then write a very brief letter to go with it, something along the lines of:

Dear [Name – James or whatever, not Mr J Smith]
I'm sending the enclosed script [title] as an example of my work. I hope you like it and will consider me as a possible writer for your series.

Yours sincerely

That is quite enough, unless you want to mention the fact that you are following up on a telephone call you've had (with that person, not with someone who merely gave you information).

Where and How to Send Out Your 'Project' Script

Things can be much more complicated with a script you're actually hoping to sell. The first thing you must realise is that the structure of television production is quite complicated. There is no such thing as 'The Television Drama Department' or 'The Television Comedy Script Department', to which you can submit scripts aimed at various programme makers, whether they are at the BBC or part of the independent sector.

The television industry is made up of several large companies that have a direct franchise (or access) to programming. These include the BBC, of course, but also several large independent companies like Granada, Channel 4, Five and others who make programmes for the various commercial channels. And these companies are generally in competition with each other. They all have a certain amount of direct access to the screen. If they like a script they can buy it in the knowledge that it will eventually be broadcast. So you can approach any one of them if you like by getting the details as before (from the *Writers' and Artists' Yearbook* or *The Writer's Handbook*).

There are also dozens of smaller independent production companies who *don't* have direct access to the screen but produce programmes for the larger companies that do, including the BBC, and you can approach any of them. So the choice is wide and potentially confusing. Luckily, you don't have to understand the process in detail, but you do need to understand it enough to ensure you don't make a fool of yourself by submitting scripts to the same destination via different routes.

Once again, you must do some research. Look closely at any sitcom or drama series that has similarities to the one you've written – it would be pretty pointless to send a thirty-minute sitcom pilot to a company that specialises in ninety-minute mini-dramas or historical epics. But whereas I've advised you to send your calling-card script out to several people at the same time, this isn't a good idea with a script you're proposing as a project in itself. Looking for an opportunity to work as a writer on someone else's series is one thing, but offering a script for sale is different. It isn't ethical to be doing this with more than one company at a time, unless you make this clear in your letter.

So you can either deal with one company at a time or send copies of the script to several companies, but make clear that that's what you are doing.

It's probably a big mistake to send copies of the same script to both the BBC and an independent company that makes programmes for the BBC (I'm sure you can see why). But it's perfectly reasonable to send copies to the BBC and also to companies that make programmes for the other channels. (Again, you can do either of these things as long as you are honest about it and let people know what you are doing.)

Be prepared to try different approaches. One of the first 'breaks' I got in writing came about when I did something that most people would tell you definitely *not* to do. I sent a rejected TV script (without altering it at all) to a radio producer, saying that the TV producer who had rejected it had made a comment about it being too wordy and more suitable for radio. I asked the radio producer if he agreed.

I did this because I was too naïve to know any better, and I got lucky because the radio producer turned out to be a decent person with a sense of humour and plenty of confidence. (It was Paul Mayhew-Archer, who was then a radio producer but who later went on to write some wonderful, top-rated shows for TV). He didn't feel insulted, as he had every right to do, at the implication that I was treating radio as an inferior medium: something I couldn't be bothered to aim at in a proper manner. He read the script, liked it, and invited me in for talks. This led to my first commission for radio, and paradoxically this eventually led right back to television.

I'm telling you this to show you that there really are no hard and fast rules. I wouldn't want to encourage you to act in this way deliberately. I got lucky. Maybe I'd have got my first break much earlier if I'd behaved with more professionalism in the first place. But sometimes you have to be as creative in trying to sell your script as you are in writing it in the first place. Just be enthusiastic and never stop trying until you are ready to admit defeat. Remember, once you have given something your best shot you can never be called a failure afterwards. You are either someone still on the way to success or you are someone who's been brave enough to try. You can't say that everybody who isn't a winner is a failure, otherwise there'd be just one successful football team in the country and all the rest would be failures. That clearly doesn't make sense. The important thing is that you do send your script out. If one approach doesn't work, try another.

The advantage of approaching a larger company directly – particularly the BBC – is that you are more likely to get an answer quickly and that they may also be more inclined to encourage a new writer. (They will have more resources and probably a better established procedure for doing these things.)

The advantage of approaching a smaller independent company is that they may be willing to suggest changes to your script in accordance with what they know about the larger companies they are dealing with. They may then suggest further changes before trying your script with other major companies.

The actual submission of your script follows the 'keep it simple' method already explained for your calling-card script. So once again it's something like:

> *Dear [Name – Jane or whatever, not Mrs J Smith]*
>
> *Please find enclosed a copy of my thirty-minute pilot episode for a proposed situation comedy series [or drama series or whatever] to be called [overall title of series].*
>
> *This episode is called [title of episode].*
>
> *I think the basic idea has lots of potential and have several further storylines which I'll be delighted to send on request.*
>
> *Yours sincerely*

That's enough. Nobody will care very much what it says in your letter; they will just want to see the script. But they might not even bother to read the script at all if your letter goes on and on and makes you appear like someone desperately looking for help. As I say, just keep it brief and businesslike.

Use the person's forename at the start of the letter and always use your own forename as well as your surname at the end of the letter. *Don't* type your name at the end of the letter as Mr or Mrs J. Brown. Scriptwriting is definitely a first name type of business: just like various sports and the acting profession. Nobody talks of Mr D. Beckham or Ms C. Zeta-Jones. Scriptwriting is the same.

It's very important to note that, if you have said you have several extra storylines, you really should have them ready just in case. You might get a phone call asking you about them, so at the very least you should have two or three at the one-page story outline stage and then a scattering of basic ideas too.

Back to submitting the actual script. Put your script and the letter in an ordinary large envelope or a suitably sized jiffy envelope and *don't* send it by registered mail or any other fancy method. Send it by ordinary first or second-class post.

If you want to be sure it's arrived it's not a bad idea to include a self-addressed and stamped postcard with your own message already written on it, saying something like 'Script arrived', with of course the name and address of the appropriate company so you'll know where it's come back from. Including your own postcard isn't *strictly* necessary, however, and the BBC in particular will usually acknowledge the arrival of a script in their own way and at their own expense.

If you want your script returned either include a SAE or enough stamps for return postage in the same envelope. I rarely bother to do this nowadays. Firstly because it's easy enough to print off extra copies, and probably not that much more expensive. Secondly because returned copies often get a bit crumpled and look as if they've been rejected, so aren't always suitable for sending out again. And thirdly because I have a naïve feeling that I'd rather have my script hanging around in someone's office, where another reader might possibly give it a second glance, than in a cupboard in my own house where it's just taking up space. (You could safely ignore this last piece of information – it's probably akin to making a wish on a dandelion clock, but you never know!) And however you look at it, sending a convenient SAE must make it so tempting, on a busy day, to stick the script inside and post it right back.

Anyway, on a purely practical level, a company will sometimes return your script even if you *haven't* included return postage. And in some senses I don't want to see a rejected script again. I don't even like the sound of that heavy clump hitting the hall floor and knowing what it is. I became so sensitive to the sound of mail arriving during my early days as a would-be writer that I swear I could lie in bed and tell the colour of an envelope from the sound it made hitting the floor. A solid clump was a rejected script, a tinny clink was a bill in a brown envelope with a window and a slightly deeper clink was a white envelope with a letter – and maybe a cheque. (It's true that my wife once asked me what sound I thought an envelope from our local psychiatric hospital might make, but that's another story.)

Just to end on a speculative note, I wouldn't be at all surprised if sending scripts by post came to an end in the not-too-distant future and it became accepted practice to make all submissions via email. Just keep an eye out for this. I'm pretty sure the *Writers' and Artists' Yearbook* and *The Writer's Handbook* will soon be including this information if they haven't already started doing so. Script layout will still be important, but you will simply send your document electronically, as an email attachment, instead of having to print it out and parcel it up.

Make a note

- Use a different approach for TV companies and agents, but always keep it simple and professional.
- Use normal postage for scripts – nothing fancy.
- Keep an eye out for the development of email submissions.

Approaching an Agent as a Novice

A third way of doing things is to approach an agent. I have to say this is probably the least effective way of doing things at this stage because successful agents aren't talent scouts. They usually represent writers who are *already* working as professionals in one field or another, negotiating contracts and so on, rather than helping people to break into the business. But you'll never know if you don't try, and here again it's a good idea to make a phone call first. This time it really is important to try and be 'yourself'. Just be *totally* honest with an agent. They are not like script-readers and script-editors who may read hundreds of scripts from people they never get to know as individuals.

An agent who considers you will want to know more about you than the fact that you can write one script. He or she will be thinking of the future: of having something more than a simple one-off business transaction with you, and in those circumstances you need to know and trust each other.

If someone at an agency says they *don't* want to see your work – believe them. You have nothing to gain by ignoring what they say and sending them your script anyway. Unlike script-readers working for a busy production company, they probably won't have dozens of scripts to read all the time. They will remember you and what they said. They are not liable to have second thoughts.

If they have any space on their books and they're suitably impressed by your confidence and ideas they have little to lose by agreeing to look at your script and might say yes to looking at it – but with absolutely no guarantees attached. They will probably ask you what other things you are interested in writing and so on and then tell you exactly what to send them.

If you don't feel confident enough to use the phone in this way by all means write to agents telling them about your script, but I wouldn't send the actual script to an agent without being invited to do so. Since they *are* interested in their clients and how they might develop, rather than in one particular script, you might as well tell them something about your ambitions in a letter. This time you can be a bit more expansive, but even so a few paragraphs on a single page is probably enough. Just tell them of any relevant successes you've had as a writer and of what you're hoping to achieve in the future. As always, keep the comments upbeat, brief, positive and polite, even if they are more personal than before. And this time you should definitely include an ordinary letter-sized SAE for a reply.

Make a note

- Send your calling-card script to any number of people you think suitable.
- Send out as many copies as you like at the same time.
- Be more specific with your 'project' script.
- Understand the difference between major production companies and others.
- Be polite and positive.
- Don't be too easily put off.
- Expect an agent to be interested in you as a person – and not just your script.

Don't Wait Around for an Answer

I remember hearing a story about a famous writer who supposedly stood up to make a speech at a writers' conference and said, 'I'm here to tell you how to become writers. Go home and write,' and then sat down again. This is probably another apocryphal story but it has more than a grain of truth in it.

Yes, there are techniques for you to learn, otherwise I wouldn't have wanted to write this book, nor would I organise workshops or talks for students. But at the very heart of things, writers write, and then write some more ... and so on. Basically the more you write the better your writing becomes and the more chance you have of selling your work. That would seem to be nothing more than common sense.

Imagine an actor doing one audition and then going home to sit by the phone waiting for an answer, or a job applicant sending out one letter and waiting patiently for a reply before trying somewhere else. It just doesn't work like that. The minute you have finished your first script and sent it out to as many people as you think necessary, you should forget about it and make a start on your next one.

Okay, I'm exaggerating again – just a little bit. Of course you won't simply be able to *forget* about it and it will certainly take much longer than a minute, but the principle holds good. Maybe you'll take a few days, or a few weeks even, to bask in the glory of having achieved something special – something you may only have dreamed about for years. You've actually completed and sent out a script that might change your life. You deserve credit for that and you *should* feel proud of yourself. Go out and celebrate if you like. But whatever you do *don't* put your creative life on hold while you wait for a decision. It will probably take several weeks, if not months, for you to get any sort of reply, and in that time your spirits could sink lower and lower if you pin too much hope on your first effort. Think how crazy that is in reality. How many people do you know who have forged a successful career after working at it for just ten weeks?

So here's what you do. You accept that you are still learning, that you are a beginner trying to carve a niche in a very competitive market. You accept that it's quite unlikely for *anyone* to make their mark with their very first attempt at something. Did Kelly Holmes become a world-class athlete in her very first race or after training for ten weeks? Of course not, nor did she expect to do so. And remember what I said much earlier: in a way you will have it harder than Kelly did at first because she would have started off competing against other novices. Right from the very beginning, you will be up against seasoned professionals.

This should excite you, not depress you, and what should excite you even more is the knowledge that it can be done. New writers are being given chances all the time, and you only have to watch a few programmes to realise that they're not all producing works of genius. Yes, there is a lot of quality drama and comedy on TV these days, despite what the cynics say, but there is also a lot of workmanlike stuff too. Do you really think it's beyond you?

So accept the fact that your first submission is likely to be less than perfect and just hope that it will be good enough to spark a show of interest from somebody. In any case, be assured that your next effort is almost certain to be better. That being the case, why not start on it more or less straight away? Then by the time you start getting rejections through the post (if that's what happens) you'll already be more focused on your second effort and maybe even the one after that. That's what real writers do. They write and they carry on writing. They don't stop at the first sign of difficulty.

Make a note

- Writers write – they don't sit around waiting for results.
- Have your next script ready to send out *before* your first one's been assessed.
- Focus more on the writing and less on the possible responses.
- Don't take a stop/go approach.
- Keep the creativity flowing.

Dealing With Outright Rejection

Suppose that all your first *and* second submissions come back with negative responses. How do you cope with that?

You simply learn what you can from any feedback and keep trying. You keep sending your latest 'calling-card' script to the shows you want to write for or you persist in looking for other outlets for your 'project' script (whilst still writing new project scripts and trying with them as well). How long you go on doing this is entirely up to you, but I can tell you that from my experiences as a teacher and speaker I find that the majority of would-be writers give up far too soon. Many of them after the very first attempt.

At the very beginning of this book I told you that the *one* thing you can't do without as a writer is persistence. I wasn't exaggerating on that point. I know people of real talent who simply can't take rejection. They would rather not even try, than try and fail. That way they don't have to face rejection and they can kid themselves that they *could* succeed if they bothered to make the effort. But they say they are too busy, or simply not interested enough, or they think that TV writing is a bit beneath them. I've heard all sorts of excuses like this, but mostly it's more to do with fear and lack of persistence than anything else.

Be brave. Be persistent. Remember that the greatest risk of all is to risk nothing, because if you risk nothing, that's what you're likely to achieve.

Suppose you send several scripts, as examples of your work, and get a response that suggests that certain companies don't want to consider any more of them? What do you do then? Well, read what they say for a start. Maybe they are right. Maybe you just don't have the right style for their show and are wasting your own time as well as theirs. But if you think they are wrong and they've made too rigid a first assessment (which can happen) there's still no need to give up.

It's a strange thing, but you have to remember that most people who work as script-readers and script-editors are unlikely to be successful writers themselves. If they were they wouldn't be *reading* scripts, they'd be writing them. This also means that they just might not understand the potential of a script as well as you do. The same goes for agents. They have other skills but they are far from infallible. Show them respect, but never allow yourself to be in awe of them.

If someone's been kind enough to give you any sort of feedback then write straight back to thank them. Tell them that you agree with their comments (if you do) and say how much you've learned from them. Then ask if you can send another script to show how much you might have improved.

If that doesn't do the trick and you eventually run out of people to keep sending scripts to (which is unlikely) you could always start using an assumed name and a friend's address, to make certain it's not become too personal. (Okay, I know this isn't being strictly honest but some people *do* use a pseudonym and use more than one address.) And you're not actually trying to cheat anybody by doing this. It's still your own script. Even if people do work out what you've done at a later date they might applaud your creativity, and isn't that what writing is all about?

Make a note

- Always have a new script on the go.
- Focus more on writing than results (at first).
- Don't take No for a final answer, Just see it as part of the negotiating procedure.
- Don't be too afraid of failure to take a risk.
- Remember that the greatest risk of all is to risk nothing.
- See the whole process as an adventure – win or lose.

More on Welcoming Feedback

As I've just said, script-readers and producers are usually busy people. They don't have time to comment on every script they see. If they do give you feedback then accept it gratefully and graciously, even if it appears to be entirely negative. A standard rejection slip tells you nothing, except that the answer is No. It might mean that nobody has even read your script. It might mean that your script is good but not the kind of thing they are looking for at that time. It might be that your script is too similar to something they already have in the pipeline – and so on. Your script can be rejected for all sorts of reasons that are nothing to do with its quality, but you will never know any of this if all you get is a rejection slip. Always remember that direct criticism, however hurtful, can teach you something (even if it's only that script-readers can make mistakes).

When you do get specific criticism take the same attitude I advised you to have when dealing with the friends who acted out your script for you. If several script-readers are highly critical of your work (and are making similar comments) then take careful note of what they're saying. If they are critical but make *differing* criticisms, then you either ignore it or decide how accurate they might still be. Never forget that creative writing isn't an exact science. To some extent it will always be a matter of taste. Even experts can get it wrong.

Many years ago I sent copies of the same sitcom script to two of the larger companies, at the same time. One sent it back saying they loved the story and thought the structure was excellent but the dialogue was too wordy. The other company said almost the exact opposite. They thought the dialogue was beautifully written but they didn't like the story or the structure. And these readers weren't beginners in the trade by any means – they were both very successful producers of sitcom.

I was a bit bemused by these conflicting comments but thrilled that they'd taken the time to make them. I wrote back straight away thanking them both, and then rewrote the script paying attention to some aspects of what they had both said. I altered the structure slightly and tightened up the dialogue, which *was* wordy, and I eventually sold the script to another producer entirely.

So however upsetting criticism might be, don't dismiss it without careful thought. Equally, don't accept it as truth either.

Make a note

- Even experts sometimes get it wrong.
- Creative writing isn't an exact science – it will always be partly a matter of taste.
- Be grateful for comments, good or bad – you can learn from them.
- From a standard rejection slip you learn virtually nothing, except that the answer isn't Yes this time!

12 Being a Writer – Not Just Playing At It

One-minute Overview

In this chapter you will learn more about behaving as a writer once you've actually sent out copies of your script. You'll realise that you need to keep on taking a professional approach if you want to avoid being constantly treated as a hopeful amateur. You'll find out why an agent might be willing to reconsider you as a client once you've made some progress and you'll be told the advantages of having an agent. You'll be told something about the pros and cons of writing with a partner. You'll be reminded about TV writing being a team effort rather than an individual one, and you'll be given more details of the people you're likely to be dealing with once your writing is taken seriously. You'll be given a warning about the changes you might expect in the way other people respond to you once they start to see you as a 'real' writer, and how best to react to this. You'll be given brief details of the kind of payments you might expect, and of certain fringe benefits you might want to pursue. Hopefully you'll be excited by it all. You should be. Working as a writer really can be as wonderful as you imagine it to be.

What Happens Next?

It's probably true to say that the vast majority of first-time scripts are returned with nothing more than a brief note of rejection. That isn't because people in general lack creative talent, it's because writing for television is harder than it looks, and most people don't take it seriously enough. You, however, have read this book and maybe other similar books too, so you start with a big advantage. You *are* taking it seriously. But you are still competing against a lot of others, including seasoned professionals, so is it realistic to hope for anything more than a word or two of encouragement at this stage? Well, actually, that's exactly what you should be *hoping* for – a letter or a phone call saying that you have great promise and someone wants to talk to you about it. Without that kind of hope what are you writing for? It *might* happen quite quickly. Some people have sold the first script they ever wrote, or at least been given the chance to write something else, that did sell, on the strength of it.

So you *hope* for instant success but you stay realistic enough to accept something less with gratitude. That something less could be, for example, a note with just a few words of encouragement, or the offer to read something else of yours. This is fine. Anything other than outright rejection is a step in the right direction and should be seized on eagerly. I repeat, be grateful to any person who has taken the time to give you some feedback. They must have thought you were worth bothering with and that means something. You are learning. You are making progress.

Never, never write back a nasty letter telling somebody exactly what you think of them and their stupid opinions. What earthly good can this do? I once sent a supposedly humorous article to a top magazine, together with a long explanatory letter saying why I'd love to write for them. I got an ever-so-slightly sarcastic reply back saying that my letter was more interesting than my article.

Instead of finding this amusing and encouraging (as it was probably meant to be and which I certainly would do if it happened now) I was deeply offended. I wrote back a petulant reply to them saying that I thought their rejection slips were more interesting than their magazine. What I said wasn't particularly funny and didn't even make sense, since I'd already told them how much I loved their magazine and that I'd be thrilled to write for it, but I was hurt and angry and reacted without thinking. See if you can guess how many articles of mine they've printed since then? (Actually it's one – but one in thirty years isn't much of a success story, is it?)

It doesn't matter who you've sent your script to or what kind of script it is: a calling-card script or a script you're hoping to sell. Nor does it matter who you've sent the script to: a soap producer, a series producer or an agent. The most likely thing to happen for a first-time writer (apart from straightforward rejection) is a few words of encouragement along with the return of your script, if you've included a SAE. Expect this but hope for something more.

One step up from this would be a phone call or letter inviting you to talk to someone or to send in more examples of your work. If this happens you really *are* getting somewhere. Once again – accept any help or advice gratefully. This is the kind of step that can lead to you being invited to write a sample script for a particular show.

As a newcomer it's unlikely you'll be paid for writing a sample script (even experienced writers only get a small token payment, if any) because your sample script has no chance of being used. You will be given detailed guidelines on what to write as a sample, which will probably be an episode that's already been written by someone else and either screened a long time ago so you won't remember it, or due to be shown in the near future so you won't have had the chance to see it.

You'll be given all the information you need to know about the episode itself and about ones that precede it or follow on from it. Then your effort will be compared with the one already written (and paid for). If you do well enough you could be commissioned to write an actual script and eventually go on to become a regular contributor to the series. (Being commissioned basically means that you'll sign a contract and get paid for whatever you do. It isn't an absolute guarantee that your script will be transmitted.)

Most writers are in this fairly precarious position. I never felt really confident that my current script would be transmitted until I was watching it on the screen, and preferably in a shop or someone else's house in case my own TV set had been rigged as part of an elaborate scam. I'm sure you've heard the old joke: 'I'm not paranoid. It's just that everybody thinks I am.' And who thought of that in the first place? A writer.

Make a note

- Don't ever write back complaining about any kind of feedback.
- Accept it with gratitude.
- Hope for instant success, but be prepared for something less.

Approaching an Agent After You've Made Some Progress

You may already have tried and failed to get an agent, but the best time to do this is when you've had some kind of offer from a production company. Even an agent who's said no to you earlier may change their mind once you've had a commission. Don't be shy about approaching them. They'll simply admire your persistence and if they don't, try elsewhere.

But do you actually *need* an agent or can you get along without one? Views differ about this. Some writers are content to handle everything by themselves, from vetting contracts to making new contacts for future projects, and others simply show their contracts to a solicitor with show-business expertise.

My own view is that a good agent can be indispensable. Yes they will take a percentage of your earnings, usually ten to fifteen per cent, but they will also drive a harder bargain than you are likely to do in the first place. The extra money they get should not only cover their costs but leave more for you as well. They are skilled negotiators and usually know what they are doing, and any future work you send out with their name on it will be treated much more seriously. As a writer friend once said on this subject, 'I'd rather have ninety per cent of *something* – than one hundred per cent of nothing.'

So it's less a question of whether you need an agent and more a question of being lucky enough to *get* one. Keep looking in one of the two reference books mentioned earlier (the *Writers' and Artists' Yearbook* or *The Writer's Handbook*) and try to choose an agent who specialises in TV scriptwriting.

Co-writing Pros and Cons

Many new scriptwriters feel uncomfortable writing alone and prefer to work with a partner. Some of the best sitcoms that we've had on our screens have been devised and written by two, or occasionally more, people working together. Galton and Simpson practically started the idea of thirty-minute sitcoms in Britain with their shows for Tony Hancock, and some memorable duos have followed them. So the idea obviously has something going for it.

It works particularly well when the two writers complement each other rather than simply duplicate each other – where one partner writes great dialogue and the other is brilliant at structure, or where one writer is good at making contacts and the other prefers to stay working hard in the background, or perhaps where one writer is male and the other female so that between them they have a better understanding of each sex. There isn't much point in writing with a partner who is exactly like yourself, though even then you can give each other encouragement.

There is a downside to writing with a partner, however. Firstly, there's the practicalities of deciding who does what. Yes, it's easy (and fun) to swap ideas but who is actually going to sit down at a keyboard and type it all out? Who is going to do most of the hard slog? And when you make cuts and changes is that same person going to do the detailed rewrites? This may seem like a very easy problem to solve between two friends. But I know from experience that it isn't. Someone who's spent a whole week re-jigging a script can easily feel resentful at a partner who then takes a few minutes to pull it all to pieces before sitting back and waiting for the next draft. Of course you can *share* the load, even if one of you is a whiz at the keyboard and the other takes a week to type out the address for an envelope, so it's not an insoluble problem – just something you need to be aware of.

A more serious situation can arise when you simply disagree over important story points, the dialogue itself or the behaviour of your shared characters. Here again some writers decide to cut out anything they're not both happy about and substitute it for something they *can* agree on (though this does smack a little of compromise, which tends to suggest something lost rather than gained). But, once again, it's not insoluble.

This leads to what I consider to be the greater risks between co-writers. Firstly, that one or the other will suddenly realise that they don't need their partner and could do it alone now that they have the confidence that comes with success. Or, conversely, that the duo isn't achieving any success and one or the other partner wants to call it a day and try writing on their own. Breaking up with a writing partner can be very similar to breaking up with any other kind of partner, including a marriage partner. And the things you've written together and not sold may become disputed items of property – like the children of divorcing parents.

I'm not talking about the scripts themselves, which you will both have access to, but of the *ideas* behind those scripts – ideas that one or the other partner may want to rework later, or characters that may still have some value if placed in another setting. Who owns these characters and ideas? This is where things can get complicated and unpleasant, especially if one or the other of you decides to take on a second writing partner who then wants to develop some aspect of your script that was previously introduced by the ex-partner.

I've had personal experience of this. I was once approached by a total stranger and asked to give an opinion on a script. Being a bit of a soft touch (at times) I agreed to do it. The script, like most untutored first-time efforts, wasn't very good, but had an interesting idea at the heart of it. I gave the person some advice and was prepared to forget all about it, but the person thanked me profusely and asked for more detailed comments. Again I complied. But then the person suggested that my name appear on the script and that we share the money if it was sold. This led to me being asked to help rewrite the whole thing, and before long I found myself taking over and changing almost everything in it. It wasn't that it was so bad, it was just like the domino theory. You push one domino over and all the rest follow until there's not one left standing.

At this point the person got angry and accused me of ruining the script. Unfortunately I had, by then, become quite fond of it and rather stupidly asked for permission to develop it alone in return for a share of any payment I might get. (I meant that this other person would be co-creator – not co-writer.) I explained that if it was ever turned into a series the co-creator would get a payment for every single episode that went out without having to do any more writing at all. The person involved got angry and threatened to sue me if I ever used *any* of the characters or situations that person had originated. My agent was also contacted and told the same thing. She was, quite rightly, furious with me and felt that as a professional with plenty of ideas of my own I should never have got involved with someone else in the first place, and especially not a new writer.

I could then see that it wasn't a very sensible thing for me to have done and that it *would* seem like a rip off to many people. I told the person involved to keep all the changes I had made and do whatever they wanted with them. I would make no claim if my revised ideas were used. I just wanted to get out of the situation with my slightly tarnished reputation for integrity intact. I don't blame the person for feeling the way they did – in their position I would probably have felt exactly the same.

So writing with a partner can be tricky. But, just as with marriage, few people would advise you not to try something that might turn out to be wonderful, just because there are risks attached. It should, in theory at any rate, be possible to reach some sort of 'pre-nuptial' agreement on all these things at the very beginning. For example, you might decide that, if you do eventually split up, you will each voluntarily relinquish control over the joint efforts you've made. In other words you give each other permission to use the characters and situations in any way you see fit without any restrictions. That seems a reasonably fair arrangement to me. You would both have the same opportunities and it seems a more sensible option than agreeing never to use them at all, because what benefit does anyone get from that?

On the other hand, you could negotiate some sort of 'created by' payment in the event of one person 'getting on' and the other 'getting left behind'. This might help to avoid the kind of bitterness and acrimony that can come with one person feeling guilty and the other feeling used.

I think my final piece of advice on this subject would have

to be: don't rush into it and, having formed a partnership, plan ahead. Don't rely on continuing goodwill, because even the nicest people can, and sometimes do, change.

If nothing else, my unhappy experience in this area taught me a valuable lesson. In the years since then I have read hundreds of scripts written by my university students and some of them have been excellent, but I have never been tempted to use any of their ideas or to suggest myself as a co-writer. I'm happy to give them as much help and encouragement as I can and wish them luck in the future.

I know by now that there's an infinite number of ideas out there. There's never any shortage. I'm hoping this book will help you realise the same and inspire you to go for it!

Make a note

- Consider things carefully before taking on a writing partner.
- Writing partners should complement and not merely duplicate each other.
- Agreement should be reached at the start over who does what (and about who owns what if and when you split up).
- It might be best to put these agreements in writing.
- Never forget that there is an infinite number of ideas in the universe (and you don't really need someone else to help you find them).

Making Friends and Keeping Them

If you do make it through to the stage where you are actually writing a commissioned script and dealing with people in a studio, be prepared for some initially tense moments. It's exciting but it can be scary too.

As I said much earlier in this book, scriptwriting is a team effort and you are quite likely to be surprised at how big that team can be. It will include script-editors, a director, a producer, a set designer, camera crew, sound engineers, wardrobe and make-up people as well as the actors. If you are using children in the cast, you may also have schoolteachers to give them lessons between takes and chaperones to look after them.

If you are joining the writing team of a soap or other long-running series you are likely to attend script conferences, with other writers and story-liners, or be at rehearsals where there might be any of the other people already listed plus others I haven't mentioned.

At one of the first rehearsals I ever attended for one of my own scripts there were over *fifty* people present. I felt nervous, but also quite proud that these important people were all there because of something I'd written down on paper. It was flattering to find myself talking to actors I'd admired for years and to answer their questions about the characters they were about to portray.

Sometimes you can be caught off guard when an actor asks a question about something you haven't even thought about. 'You know when James rushes out of the house slamming the door behind him? Where does he go to?' That's when you have to think quickly, because it's not a good idea to say, 'Who cares? I just needed to get him out of the way so that his wife can make a phone call.' That's when you either have a flash of inspiration and say something like, 'Oh, didn't I make it clear that he always goes for a walk by the canal when he's upset?' Or simply admit that you hadn't really thought about it and then ask the actor what he or she thinks.

At first I would feel irritated and a bit threatened by questions like this, but I quickly came to realise that the actors who were asking these questions were usually the ones who were taking the whole thing really seriously and coming up with the best performances. On top of which they were paying me a compliment by expecting me to 'know' my characters better than they did, at least at the beginning.

It's also possible to become frustrated by script-editors, producers and directors who might insist on changes you really don't like, but as I said before, you have sold your script and it isn't really your property anymore. The important thing for you to remember in these circumstances is to stay calm and be friendly. In some ways this is a small industry and people do sometimes move around from one studio to another and from one series to another. Get yourself a bad reputation and it won't remain a secret for long. That doesn't mean you can never stand up for yourself, of course. It just means that you do it sensibly and reasonably. People will respect you for having strong opinions, but not for trying to force them on others by being angry or sulky.

More on the Personnel and Their Roles

Near the beginning of the book I told you very briefly something about the people you'll have to deal with, once your work starts to get taken seriously. I also promised to elaborate on this, so here goes:

Script-reader

This remains, as I said before, simply a term to denote a person who is reading your script *before* it's been accepted. It might, in a large company like the BBC, be an actual 'reader' who does nothing else but pass an initial judgement on a script, but it's more likely to be someone who is also a script-editor or a producer.

Script-editor

This is the person you are likely to have the most dealings with. The script-editor works closely with the writer, going over the script scene by scene and word by word. It's their job to make sure that what you have written is not only as good as you can get it artistically but also that it's well-written *technically.*

They help you make sure that your script isn't impossible to shoot, and that it fits into the series as a whole, within the available budget. They will also understand any other constraints to do with time limits or actors availability, for example.

Script-editors will often act as a buffer between you and everyone else involved, including the producer, director, location managers, set designers and actors. You really must strive to get along with them. This doesn't mean you have to slavishly take on board everything they say, but it does mean you have to treat their opinions with respect.

Director

As already explained, the director is the person who works with the actors and the various technicians to turn your script into a TV show. The director may want to talk to you about various aspects of your script but will probably be wary of treading on the toes of the script-editor and making suggestions that go against something the script-editor has asked you to do. He or she is likely to ask for the script-editor's approval before talking to you. As I said much earlier, it's a real team effort and there needs to be an accepted chain of command that everyone understands.

Producer

The producer is actually the boss. Everybody else is subordinate to him or her. You will probably meet the producer before meeting the director (especially if you have managed to sell your script as a one-off or a pilot for your own series).

Sometimes the producer will relay comments to you through the script-editor, and sometimes he or she will deal with you directly. These direct comments are likely to be more general than those of the script-editor, but they are also likely to be less open to discussion. The producer has the most power and probably won't talk to you about anything other than major issues. He or she will expect the others, already mentioned, to help you with the precise details.

Actors

The actors are quite likely to ask questions of you if they get the chance, but similarly they don't want to cause confusion or animosity by doing this out of turn. The general rule seems to be that the actors will talk to the director first, then the script-editor and finally the writer.

It's quite important that the writer and script-editor should present a pretty united front towards everyone else once they have made firm decisions on the script. For them to start arguing at this stage could cause chaos. Similarly, the director is liable to be very upset if a writer, script-editor or even producer starts interfering with his or her suggestions to the actors, on how they should 'play' a scene or whatever. Each person has a job to do and it isn't always easy to see where the boundaries between these jobs lie. As I've already said, it needs teamwork.

So if you thought the writer's job begins and ends at his own desk, you can see you were mistaken. You also have to be a salesperson and a diplomat.

Make a note

- A writer's job doesn't end when the script is put in the post.
- A writer needs to be a salesperson and a diplomat.
- There is a chain of command to be observed in a studio.
- People have their own specific roles to fulfil.
- Roles can sometimes overlap, so care is needed.

People Trying to 'Sell' You Ideas

Another thing (similar to co-writing) that will almost certainly happen to you once you've had some success is that people will come to you with ideas. That's fine if they just offer to give you the idea and leave it at that, but sometimes they will suggest you can use their idea at a price. They don't seem to realise that writing is hard work, so they will say something like this: 'I'll tell you my brilliant idea – you write the script and we'll split the profits fifty-fifty.'

The last time someone offered to do this with me I politely stopped him short and asked him what he did for a living. He said he was a builder. I told him that was interesting because I had a brilliant idea for a house. I would draw it on a piece of paper and he would build it. Then we'd share the profits fifty-fifty. He wasn't interested and went away thinking I was a bit odd, but he didn't accuse me of trying to pinch his idea because I never got to hear it – thank goodness.

You must take a similar attitude. Don't give any support to people who think that professional scriptwriting is easy and it's just the ideas that really count. Make it clear to them that it's usually the other way around.

- Most people don't think that writing is a 'real' job.
- They think that anybody could do it with a bit of help.
- They are wrong on both counts.
- Don't get involved with such people.

Getting the 'Right' Attitude

I've already said that the one thing you can't do without as a would-be writer is persistence. No doubt you've noticed how often I've repeated various things throughout this book, which is a form of persistence in itself (so let that be a lesson to you!). But of course you don't want your persistence to go too far and turn into unpleasant pushiness. You need to pay attention to your overall attitude.

One excellent way to improve your chances of success as a writer is by reading books on positive thinking. One useful strategy I learned from such books is that if you ever find yourself in an unpleasant situation it's a good idea to stop thinking about who's winning the argument and concentrate on what you want to get out of it. It sounds very simple but it really works. Stop trying to score points. Ignore any insults, insofar as this is possible, and politely but firmly keep stating your views in a reasonable and friendly manner. In other words, focus on your positive *actions* and ignore your negative *reactions.*

You still may not get what you want on this particular occasion, but you should have avoided making an enemy and it's more than likely you'll have gained the kind of respect that will be useful at a later date.

Notice that I've continually used the word 'persistence' with regard to your own attitude rather than the word 'determination' throughout this book. There's a reason for this. I always think of determination as more ruthless than persistence. It goes with the word 'grim', as in 'grim determination', and suggests the actions of someone who is going to win at all costs, no matter who gets hurt in the process. (That's why I've used 'determination' sometimes to describe the actions of characters in a drama. I don't mind *them* causing trouble! It helps the drama.)

Persistence, on the other hand, suggests a willingness to keep trying, perhaps accepting advice in the process, without bitterness. To me this is altogether less threatening and more inclusive. I've found books on positive thinking very useful in this respect and suggest that you might do the same.

Lots of books on positive thinking, probably listed under 'self help', are being published at the moment so choosing a particularly appropriate one for yourself isn't that easy. I'd suggest you start by reading a few from your local library first and then see what you think of them. I could tell you right now how reading such books totally changed my life, but that's a completely different story. I'll just say that my own favourites include: *The Sky's the Limit* by Wayne Dyer, *Bring Out the Magic in your Mind* by Al Koran (if you ignore the self promotion), *Awaken the Giant Within* by Anthony Robbins, *Feel the Fear and do it Anyway* by Susan Jeffers and some much older ones by pioneers in the subject like Dale Carnegie, Napolean Hill and W. Clement Stone.

(Author's note: Since the first edition of this book my own book on self-help has been published. It's called: *Choose Happiness. Ten steps to bring the magic back into your life*, published by Aber Publishing. Since it was positive thinking that helped me become a writer in the first place this might be a particularly appropriate book for me to recommend to anyone reading this book. Not surprisingly, I'm happy to do that.)

Make a note

- Stay on good terms with people in the studio.
- This is a relatively small world you're trying to enter.
- Focus on what you want to gain from a discussion – not on winning the argument.
- Check out some of the books on positive thinking in your local library.

Payment and Fringe Benefits

Rates of pay can vary quite a lot for freelance scriptwriters, but the good news is that they are likely to be high compared with many other forms of writing.

An established writer will get more than a newcomer and ITV companies usually pay more than the BBC. You will get more when writing for a series where you provide your own main storyline, than for one where you don't. You might also get a contract that either promises you royalties for repeat showings in this country and abroad, or a lump sum in lieu of this. That's another good reason why you'll probably need the advice of an agent or a solicitor before signing a contract, to see that things such as royalties and overseas payments are covered.

There is even a company in this country that monitors overseas payments and royalties in general and tries to make sure that writers don't lose out. It's called the Authors' Licensing and Collecting Society Limited (ALCS) and seems to me to do a wonderful job.

To check what the current rates of payment are likely to be for scriptwriters look again at a current issue of the *Writers' and Artists' Yearbook* or *The Writer's Handbook.* As a very rough guide, even beginners can expect to be paid something in excess of £100 per minute of screen time, and experienced writers much more than this. Many comedy scriptwriters I know, including some beginners, were getting that kind of money, plus repeat fees, as far back as the early 1990s. (On the other hand, comedy writing is one of the more highly-paid areas of scriptwriting – so you will need to check for yourself.)

As well as any royalties you *may* get over the years there are certain other fringe benefits on offer for scriptwriters. I once had my own regular slot on a local radio station, writing and presenting my own material, and I've sold several articles to magazines. Of course this kind of thing can happen to you, too, once you've made the initial breakthrough.

You might also, for example, be offered the chance to give talks to writers' groups – either locally or at various writers' holidays or conferences. My own personal favourite, from the point of view of both tutor and student, is the annual writers' holiday held in Caerleon in Wales. The atmosphere is relaxed and friendly, the food and accommodation are excellent and the writing courses are all run by practising writers who are successful in their own field. You can easily check out their website by typing 'Caerleon Writers' Holiday' into your search engine.

Two other writers' events I can personally recommend are the annual Writers' Summer School at Swanwick and the ones organised by the National Association of Writing Groups (NAWG). Details of these can also be found quite easily on the internet.

You might want to consider going to one of these places as a student and then imagine how it might feel to be invited back later as a successful writer (and get paid for it!). It can and does happen. Apart from a few regular tutors, who are rotated year by year anyway, there is always a demand for new ones. Why not you? Lots of the excellent speakers and tutors who now appear at one or another of these places made their first visit to a writers' event as a student.

Some successful writers can also earn large sums of money by joining the after-dinner speaking circuit, which is another story and another skilled craft to learn. But it can be done and, unlike scriptwriting, you can start off in a small way and build upwards. Start with small groups, like writing groups or Women's Institutes, in your own area and see how it goes. It can be enjoyable and give you a bit of extra pocket money, if nothing else.

I hope that learning about such possibilities has increased your desire to really make it as a professional writer. To paraphrase something I said a little earlier in this book, 'anybody can'. So long as they work hard at it and *persist.* But this book is really about writing your *first* TV script so let's get back to that with the details given in the following pages – and good luck!

Appendix

Acceptable Script Layout

There are many variations of acceptable script layout, with minor differences, but the one shown here is as good as any and very easy to use if you follow these instructions. I'm assuming you will be using a modern computer with a Microsoft Word program. In the following pages you'll be told exactly how to set up these specifications so you can use them easily and quickly.

The Basics

- Use white A4 copier paper 80gsm.
- Use Times New Roman as type style.
- Use font size 12.
- Print on only one face of each page.
- Start with a title page (using normal margin settings).
- Follow that with a very short blurb about your story as a whole (using normal margin settings)
- Follow that with a brief character list on third page (using normal margin settings).
- Begin actual script on third page, after resetting margins:
  – left margin 6cm
  – right margin 2cm.
- Number your pages in bottom right hand corner.
- Start every scene on a new page.
- Punch a single hole through every page in top left-hand corner and fasten with a split-pin or stationery tag fastener.

Example of Title Page

Your address
Phone number
Email

TITLE (capitals and bold)
by
Your name (John Smith, not Mr J Smith)
Very brief description of what it is – a thirty-minute drama – or a thirty-minute sitcom.

Example of Blurb

SUCCESS STORY is a comedy with a serious theme – of corruption and temptation.

JAMES FOSTER and his wife KATE are struggling but honest. JAMES is a schoolteacher in a primary school and going nowhere slowly. KATE is a housewife who gave up her chance of a career to raise a family. Now they're grown-up she feels that life has moved on and left her with little chance of catching up.

ALBERT FOSTER is JAMES'S older brother. He and MIRIAM, his attractive no nonsense wife, are rich and amoral. They left their home town some years before to seek richer pickings elsewhere and have made their money in various shady ways but they are generous outgoing people who enjoy life to the full.

In the past KATE and MIRIAM were 'best' friends who met the brothers on a mutual date. MIRIAM still likes KATE and feels sorry for her. She and ALBERT would love to help KATE if only KATE would accept their help and JAMES would 'allow' it.

Fate takes a hand when a death in the family throws the two couples together and KATE becomes involved with MIRIAM and ALBERT in a local business venture.

JAMES doesn't like it one little bit but that won't deter MIRIAM and ALBERT because they love a challenge and they intend to spend a lot more time in the area…

(Author's note: This is a copy from one of my own scripts so the names won't tally with the character names on the next page. You can see that I'm trying to 'sell' the idea as a series – not just this pilot script).

Example of Character List Page

Character list

John Smith..45

Wendy Smith (John's partner) 45

Simon Smith (their son) 9

Ann Jones..35

Ben Williams 74

(And so on – just giving the bare details of the main characters, not their descriptions and perhaps ending with the number of speaking and NSEs (non-speaking extras like bar staff or waiters – people who actually interact with the main characters and will be noticed rather than simply making up the background.)

Example of Script Beginning

Address etc

TITLE

SCENE I. EXT. SMITH'S HOUSE. DAY.

[A SIMPLE ESTABLISHING SHOT OF A LARGE DETACHED HOUSE IN AN AFFLUENT AREA OF A LARGE ENGLISH CITY. THERE'S A BRAND NEW PORSCHE ON THE DRIVEWAY AND THE GARDEN IS IMMACULATE.]

CUT TO:

SCENE 2. INT. SMITH'S HOUSE LOUNGE. DAY.

[JOHN SMITH, AN ATTRACTIVE AND CHARISMATIC MAN OF 45, IS SITTING IN AN ARMCHAIR READING A NEWSPAPER. THE FURNITURE AND FITTINGS ARE STYLISH AND EXPENSIVE.

A PHONE ON A NEARBY TABLE RINGS. JOHN THROWS HIS NEWSPAPER TO ONE SIDE AND REACHES EAGERLY FOR THE RECEIVER.]

JOHN:

(INTO PHONE) Hello ... (QUIETER) Ann ... is it you?

[A DOOR OPENS AND WENDY SMITH, JOHN'S PARTNER, COMES IN. SHE IS A STRIKINGLY ATTRACTIVE WOMAN OF 45.]

WENDY:

John I was just wondering if ... Oh ... sorry dear, I didn't ...

JOHN:

(SMILING) It's only Ben ... you know ... from the golf club ...

(And so on ...)

Script Formatting

These notes include directions on how to achieve the suggested layout by using shortcut keys. Don't be put off by the fact that it looks complicated. It only takes a few minutes to set up and can save you countless hours once you start using it. You will be able to change the position of text on the page, add underlining, change case and type letters in bold at a stroke by using shortcut keys.

These instructions apply specifically to Microsoft Word, but no doubt something similar may apply to other programs – or you may prefer to buy a special scriptwriting program with various formats built into it to add to your computer.

Meanwhile, try this system and see. Please note: (it is important that you do these set ups in the order shown).

Title page and character list page

Unless you have changed the settings on your computer already, it will probably have the following as the default settings:

Typestyle – Times New Roman

Font size – 12

Paper size – A4

Orientation – Portrait

If not, set them now.

Type style and font size can clearly be seen on your regular toolbar. Click on these to change them if necessary.

To change **paper size** and **orientation** do the following:

Click **file** on toolbar.

Click on **page setup**.

Click on **paper size** tab.

Set the following:
Paper size – A4
orientation – portrait

Click **OK** box.

Use the above settings for your normal everyday writing, including the first three pages of your script – the title example page, the blurb example page and the character list example page.

Apply page break.

For the rest of the script following the page break – do this:

Margins for script layout

Click on **file** on toolbar.

Click on **page setup**.

Click on the **margins** tab.

Set the following:
top – 2.5cm
bottom – 2.5cm
left – 6cm
right – 2cm
gutter – 0cm
header – 1.25cm
footer – 1.25cm
apply to: this point forward (to protect title page and character list page)

Character names before dialogue

For example:

JOHN:

Type in your first **character name** (in ordinary text) and highlight with mouse.

On the toolbar click on **format**.

Click on **style**.

Click on **new box**.

In the **name box** type 'Character'.

In the **style for following paragraph** box set it for **normal** (this will automatically take care of the dialogue to follow character names so long as you press enter and start dialogue *below* the character name as in script example).

Click on **format box** and then click on **font**.

Set the following:

font – Times New Roman
font Style – bold
size – 12
underline – single
effects – all caps

Click on **OK**.

Click on **shortcut key** box

Press **Alt** and **C** keys together. (This will set up a shortcut key. Simply press **Alt** and **C** every time you want to type in *any* character name as appropriate. If you forget to do this you can highlight names with the mouse and then press **Alt** and **C** together.)

Click **assign**.

Click **close**.

Click **OK**.

Click **apply.**

Directions

All directions should be in capital letters, with different margins from scene headings and dialogue. They should also be enclosed in square brackets. For example:

> [JOHN SITS ON CHAIR READING A NEWSPAPER.]

(Use *curved* brackets elsewhere in the script, as shown in the script example.)

Type in your first **direction** (in normal text and position) and highlight with the mouse.

On the toolbar click **format**.

Click on **style**.

Click on **new box**.

In the **name box** type 'Directions'.

Click on the **format box** and then on **font**. Set the following:

font – Times New Roman
font style – regular
size – 12
underline – none

effects – all caps

Click on **OK**.

Click on **format**.

Click on **paragraph**.

Set the **left indentation** at 2.5cm. All other settings should remain at zero. Line spacing should be set at single.

Click on **OK**.

Click on **shortcut key box**.

Press **Alt** and **D** together. (This has set up a shortcut key for directions. Simply press **Alt** and **D** together before typing in directions – or highlight with the mouse afterwards and press **Alt** and **D** together.)

Click **assign**.

Click **close**.

Click **OK**.

Click **apply**.

Scene headings

All scene headings should be in capital letters, bold and underlined, for example:

SCENE I. EXT. SMITH'S HOUSE. DAY.

Type in first **scene heading** (in normal text and position) and highlight with the mouse.

On the toolbar click **format**.

Click on **style**.

Click on **new box**.

In the **name box** type 'Scene Heading'.

Click on the **format box** and then on **font**. Set the following:

font – Times New Roman
font style – Bold
size – 12
underline – single
effects – all caps

Click on **OK**.

Click on **shortcut key box**.

Press **Alt** and **S** together. (This has set up a shortcut key for scene headings. Simply press **Alt** and **S** together before typing in scene headings – or highlight with the mouse afterwards and press **Alt** and **S** together.)

Click **assign**.

Click **close**.

Click **OK**.

Click **apply**.

Cut to

All scenes should finish with CUT TO in capital letters. This should be bold, underlined and followed by a colon, exactly like your scene headings:

CUT TO:

Since this *is* the same as the layout for scene headings you can simply use **Alt** and **S** together for this as well as scene headings. There is no need to set up another shortcut key. It's also convenient that scene headings follow cut tos in all but the initial case, which means you don't even have to press the scene-heading shortcut key most of the time. It will already be set up from the cut to.

The one tiny problem with this is that if you want to type the word 'Finish' at the end of your script it will come out in the same style as your scene headings and cut tos:

FINISH

There's nothing wrong with that of course – except that you might also want to add your name and address to the bottom of the final page too – and that would look a bit silly in this style. In that case you can simply press **Alt** and **C** together to format the Character names style (which you'll remember is followed by normal) type out a few letters and then press enter. Then after typing your name and address a few spaces below this you can simply delete the letters typed in bold and underlined.

If, on the other hand, you've concluded the action with a line of dialogue there's no problem. You simply drop down a space or two, type the word 'Finish' and heave a satisfied sigh of relief – as I've just done.

May I once again wish you good luck and urge you always to remember the magic word – persistence.

Index

More titles for the Creative Writer

Writing Science Fiction 'What if…!'

Who else wants to write science fiction?
Written by professional writer (see www.lazette.net/) this book takes the reader by the hand and explains exactly how to create a commercially successful science fiction novel. The author is well known in the genre and regularly teaches creative writing. This book defines science fiction and explains the different categories of science fiction. The reader is then taught the basics of research, how to build a world based on science and myth, how to build 'the others', namely building up believable characters in your Aliens, how to write the language of the future, placing stories in the universe, space travel, the possibilities of government in the future, the challenge of writing something new, creating an effective outline, being a professional writer and preparing your manuscript for the publisher.

Lazette Gifford is a name in science fiction circles. She lives with her husband and family in the USA where she is a prolific writer, photographer and computer generated artist.

Author Lazette Gifford | **Price** £10.99 €12.99 | **Format** Paperback, 215 x 135mm, 160pp

ISBN 978-1-84285-060-2

Kate Walker's 12 Point Guide to Writing Romance

Here is how to become a published romance writer
If you want to write romance and be a professional writer then this book is a must for you. Following on from the success of the first edition of this book, which won a major award, this guide explains what is meant by romance and takes you through the process of writing emotion and conflict. The author explains how dialogue should be natural between your heroine and her hero and she explains the difference between sensuality and passion. With an expanded text and more true insider-secrets this is a must for all writers of romance, whether professional or amateur.
In this book you will learn:

- How to write emotion and create PTQ (page turning quality).
- Why dialogue is the lifeblood of your novel.
- The importance of 'after'.
- Why the intense black moment is so important.

Kate Walker has published in over 50 countries and has sold over 15 million romance novels worldwide.

Author Kate Walker | **Price** £10.99 €12.99 | **Format** Paperback, 215 x 135mm, 160pp

ISBN 978-1-84285-128-9

Writing Historical Fiction -

Creating the historical blockbuster

Who else wants to become a top selling novelist?

Have you always wanted to write historical fiction but not known how to go about it? Or are you a published novelist who wants to switch genres? In her meticulously researched book – packed with worked examples, summaries and tips - Marina Oliver covers all aspects of writing historical fiction –

This book includes details on:

- ten things you need to do to get started
- how to research your target period
- presenting your work to a publisher or agent
- the 5 stages of a plot
- how to write convincing dialogue
- the publication process

Marina Oliver has published over 50 historical novels and is a well-known teacher of creative writing.

Author Marina Oliver | **Foreword** Richard Lee Founder of the Historical Novel Society
Price £10.99 **€**12.99 | **Format** Paperback, 215 x 135mm, 160pp

ISBN 978-1-84285-077-0

Writing 'how-to' articles and books

How to share your know-how and get published

Here is how to be a successful non-fiction writer

Who else wants to use their knowledge and experience to write non-fiction articles and books?

It really could be you! Just imagine, with a little bit of guidance you really could have your book on the bookshelves of national and even international chains of bookshops. This book will show you how to achieve it.

In this book Chris McCallum explains how to:

- Assess your knowledge and experience.
- Write 'how-to' articles.
- Write for magazines.
- Survive and succeed in today's publishing world.
- Break in with tips and fillers.
- Approach your market.
- Write a 'how-to' book.

Chriss Mc Callum has over 30 years of experience in the book trade both as a writer and as a publishing executive.

Author Chriss McCallum | **Price** £10.99 €12.99 | **Format** Paperback, 215 x 135mm, 240pp

ISBN 13 978-1-84285-095-4

Writing Crime Fiction -

Making Crime Pay

Information Points

- Written by an expert who is a published crime writer
- Deals with a growing market of amateurs and undergraduates
- Each chapter develops a mental or practical skill
- Advice packaged in bite-sized chunks.

Here is how to become a published crime writer

Writing crime is an excellent introduction to the genre from a well-established and highly respected author.

Foreword by International Best-selling author Val McDermid

In this book you will learn:

- How to start writing crime
- How to layer your novel with clues
- How to find a market for your work
- How to be a professional crime writer

Janet Laurence is an established crime writer. She is the author of the *Darina Lisle* crime series and the *Canaletto* murder series and the novel *To Kill the Past.* She is also the writer in residence at a college in Australia every summer. Janet Laurence lives in Somerset where like her heroine she enjoys cooking.

Author Janet Laurence | **Price** £10.99 **€**12.99 | **Format** Paperback, 215 x 135mm, 160pp

ISBN 13 978-1-84285-088-6

Starting to Write: Step-by-step guidance to becoming an author

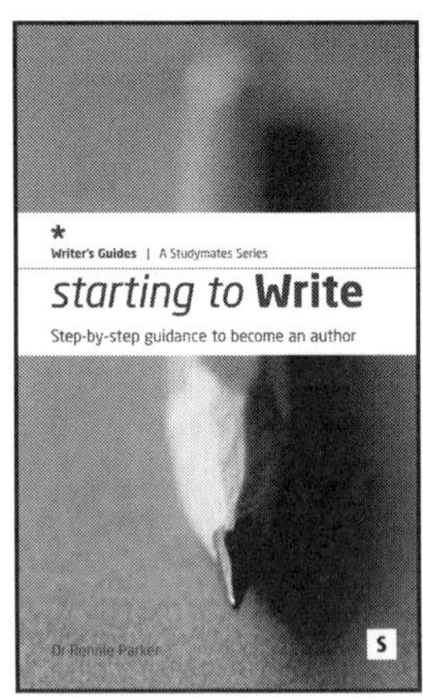

Information Points

- Written by an expert academic who is also a published writer
- Deals with a growing market of amateurs and undergraduates
- Each chapter develops a mental or practical skill
- Advice packaged in bite-sized chunks.

Here is how to become a published writer

Many people yearn to become a published writer but publishers complain of the poor quality manuscripts they receive and how they are un-publishable. There are a substantial number of novice writers who are making totally avoidable mistakes.

In this book you will learn:

- How to start writing and become your best critic
- How to deal with writers block, rejection and still keep writing
- How to find a market for your work
- How to find the best writing style and best area to write in, for your personality.

Chriss Mc Callum has over 30 years of experience in the book trade both as a writer and as a publishing executive.

Author Dr Rennie Parker | **Price** £10.99 €12.99 | **Format** Paperback, 215 x 135mm, 160pp

ISBN 978-184285-093-0

Writing and Imagery

How to deepen creativity and improve your writing

Information Points

- Creative writing is one of the fastest-growing reader groups in the UK.
- Potential to market through the network of writers' groups and specialist writing press.
- Author is a 'name' in creative writing, regularly leads creative writing classes and is credited with finding a new talent Mark Lawrence of Prince of Thorns.

Here is how to use creativity to improve your writing
Written by professional writer and very experienced creative writing teacher, this book explains the nature of creativity and how a basic understanding of the brain function can enhance the creative process. This book explains how through cultural shifts, the use of imagery has become more mainstream in the last 25-years and how this is a jumping off point to using creative imagery to reframe writing for different markets.

Author Ann Palmer | **Price** £10.99 **€**12.99 | **Format** Paperback, 215 x 135mm, 160pp

ISBN 978-1-84285-061-9

Writing Soap: How to write Continuous Drama

Information Points

- Authoritative - written by a very experienced radio and tv writer
- A growing market of creative writers ready to snap up this book.
- Huge market- there are many thousands of novice creative writers in the UK alone

Who else wants to write for the 'soaps'?
'Soaps' like *Eastenders, Coronation Street, Emmerdale, Casualty, Holby City*, and of course the ever-popular *Archers* on BBC Radio 4 all need new storylines to keep them fresh and that means new writers. It really could be your lines being uttered by an actor in a scene on tv or radio.

This book explains how:

- continuous drama is made and the role of the script writer
- to write for established characters in a 'soap'
- to develop your writing style so that it becomes compelling writing

Author Chris Thompson | **Price** £11.99 €12.99 | **Format** Paperback, 215 x 135mm, 160pp

ISBN 13 978-1-84285-118-0